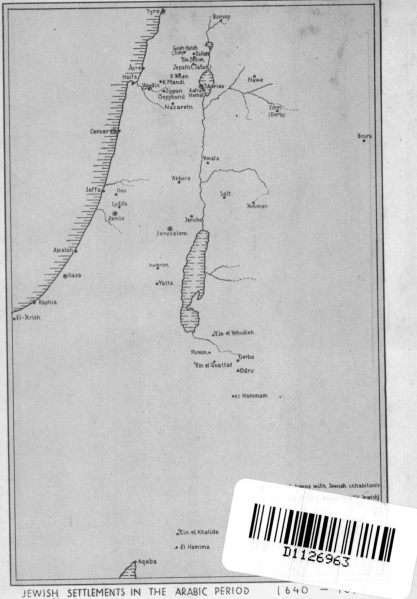

Tyre
Banyas
Gush-Halab (Jish) Dalkah
Ein Zetim
Zepath (Safad)
Acre
Haifa K'Aran
K. Mandi Nawe
'Ibellin
Zippori (Sepphoris) Kafra
(Sepphoris) Hamat Tiberias
Nazareth
Edrei (Dera)
Caesarea
Bosra
'Amata
'Akbara
Jaffa Ono
Salt
Lydda
Ramle Amman
Jericho
Jerusalem
Ascalon
hebron
Gaza Yatta
Raphia
El-'Arish

'Ein el Yehudieh
Punon Gerba
'Ein el Quattat Odru

El Hammam

towns with Jewish inhabitants
(... Jewish)

'Ein el Khalida
El Hamima

D1126963

Aqaba

JEWISH SETTLEMENTS IN THE ARABIC PERIOD (640 —
Aa known from contemporary documents and literature.

THE AUTHOR

BERL LOCKER CLAIMS to be "an elderly gentleman of 60." Nobody who knows the puckish good humor and irrepressible spirits of this scholar and political leader will believe this description. His youthfulness belies the statistics of his career, which show that he joined the Labor Zionist Movement (Poale Zion) almost at its inception in 1905, that he was a leading figure, as editor and party worker, in Lwow, Poland (1911), The Hague in Holland (1916), New York (1928), London (1931), and Tel-Aviv (1935). Since 1938, when he returned to London as Political Adviser of the Jewish Agency, of whose Executive he is a long-standing member, he has been responsible for conducting the relations of the Zionist Movement with the British Government, and particularly with the British Labor Party. In the midst of this busy and productive career, he has continued to write articles and books, combining scholarship with his own light and lucid touch.

COVENANT
Everlasting

PALESTINE IN JEWISH HISTORY

By Berl Locker

❧

SHARON BOOKS

1947

NEW YORK

To Chaim Weizmann

TABLE OF CONTENTS

INTRODUCTION

THIS VOLUME SHOULD *be required reading for all who speak or write on the problem of Palestine. It is the convincing answer to those who argue that the Jews have no special historical claim in the Holy Land. Through pertinent citations of historical texts and a logical re-appraisal of the millennial story of Jews in Palestine, Mr. Locker makes his case.*

As a Christian, I am repeatedly shocked by the casual, almost callous, acceptance by Christian leaders, including many in the Ministry who should, of course, know better, of the current misinterpretations of the Jewish people's relation to Palestine. Surely the least that a non-Jew can do is to be objective in his statements about the Jews' historic role in Palestine. The reading of Mr. Locker's little book will help not alone the non-Jews, but also those Jews who are ignorant of their own past, to understand why there can be no substitute for Palestine in the aspirations of the Jewish people.

MAY 9, 1947   JAMES G. MCDONALD

Author's Preface

THE HISTORICAL connection of the Jewish people with Palestine—internationally recognized by the Mandate —is a strange and unique phenomenon. It has no parallel in the history of any other people. It cannot be explained by comparison and generalization. *Clichés* are useless. No wonder that very few people have any true conception of the real meaning of this historical connection and its full implications. Most people regard it as a pale vestige of past history, or at best as an eschatological conception which is concerned only with the "world to come" and not at all with the acute problems of the present.

This misapprehension is taken advantage of by opponents of Zionism. The thirteen hundred years that have passed since the Moslem conquest of the country are represented as a period of uninterrupted residence by the descendants of the first invaders. All the upheavals and destructions caused by the dynastic wars, the Crusades, the invasions by Carmathians, Kharezmians, Seldjuk Turks, Mongols, and by Turkish rule are ignored. On the other hand, the eighteen hundred years since the destruction of the Second Temple and of the Jewish state in 70 C.E. are regarded as marking an era throughout which the real ties between the Jewish people and its ancient homeland were completely severed. All that is conceded is a "spiritual connection," or at best that the Jews love Jerusalem "as the Roman Catholic loves Rome, or the Australian the mother country." See for example Maude Royden, in *The Problem of Palestine* (Hutchinson, 1939). There, after discussing the "claim that Jehova promised it to them" and dismissing it as "begging the question," the Christian Doctor of Divinity rejects the historical right of the Jews to Palestine.

Attack upon the historical connection of the Jewish people with Palestine and their historical right to the country is at present developing simultaneously in two dimensions—time and space. The length of the Jewish people's residence in Palestine is now shortened not only at its latter end—the destruction of its statehood—but also at its beginning. At the same time, the area of Jewish domination is reduced to insignificant proportions.

"The ancient Hebrews never occupied much that the Jews now claim; they only passed through Transjordan and they only raided Galilee (rightly called by them 'of the Gentiles') and Philistia, and they held what they occupied for scarcely 500 years." (Dr. G. R. Driver in a letter to *The Times,* October 10, 1945.) Dr. Driver digresses even into the field of racialism: "The Jews," he says, "are no more Hebrews than the Italians are Romans, and their racial claim to Palestine is no stronger than an Italian claim to Britain would be—except for the senti-

10

mental appeals whipped up by Zionism."

While the historical contentions of Dr. Driver are fully answered in the text of this book, it may not be superfluous to deal here briefly with his geographical "discoveries." The Jews had not "only passed through Transjordan." Bashon was occupied by the half-tribe of Manasseh, and though conquered in the ninth century B.C. by the Syrian Hazael, it was reconquered by Jerobeam II (II *Kings,* 14, 25). In later times it was conquered by the Nabataeans. Gilead, the territory between the rivers Yarmuk in the north and Arnon in the south, constituted the Eastern domain of Israel. (George Adam Smith, *Historical Geography of the Holy Land,* p. 578)

The Jews had not "only raided Galilee," The tribes of Asher, Naphtali, Zebulun and a portion of the tribe of Dan were settled there. The expression "Galilee of the Gentiles" was originally only "applied to the northern border of Israel, which was pressed and permeated from three sides by foreign tribes," but it did not mean that the whole region which was later covered by the name of Galilee was not Jewish. True, after the return from Babylonian captivity Jews for a considerable time formed a minority in Galilee, but in the second century B.C. the region was finally reconquered and soon afterwards Galilee was "thoroughly Jewish" and "had developed a loyalty to the Jewish state sufficient to throw off a strong invader" (l.c., p. 414).

The role of Galilee in the struggle for Jewish independence and in the spiritual life of the nation in later centuries is discussed in chapters X-XV.

That the Philistines were never definitely subdued until the Babylonian captivity is, to be sure, correct. But the Philistines disappeared long before the Arab conquest, and Jewish settlements continued to exist for centuries in Jabne, Gaza, Rafa, Aqaba and elsewhere on formerly Philistine territory.

Along somewhat the same lines as Dr. Driver, Mr. Richard Stokes, M.P., an arden Roman Catholic, makes this definite statement: "About 900 B.C. the Israelites occupied that part of it [Palestine] which might be roughly called Judea. They were turned out in A.D. 70 by the Romans and in A.D. 632 it was conquered by the Arabs, who have lived there ever since." (*Daily Herald*, October 18, 1945)

Mr. Thomas Reid, M.P., adorned the debate on Palestine in the House of Commons (21st February, 1946) with a similar contribution of historical scholarship.

The apex of originality, however, was attained by His Majesty King Ibn-Saud of Arabia, who, in a letter to the late President Roosevelt dated March 10, 1945, wrote that the Canaanites, "an Arab tribe which emigrated from the Arab Peninsula," lived in Palestine 3,500 years before the Christian era, whereas the Jews altogether spent in the country "380 confused and sporadic years."

Such quotations could be prolonged *ad infinitum*. But these suffice to show the need for a serious though short discussion of the historical aspect of the relationship between the people and the land of Israel. It is not my intention to write another textbook; the only purpose of this little book is to trace those phenomena in Jewish history—and their connection with world history—which prove or illustrate the living meaning of the term "historical connection" of the Jewish people with Eretz Israel. It consists, therefore, rather of glimpses than of a continuous narrative of the different aspects of historic events and developments. It does not claim to have brought to light much new historical material. Most of the facts and events discussed are known, but are not always adequately correlated by historians. I have quoted as far as possible from books accessible to the English reader, though I owe much to works in other languages, especially to the labors of Jewish historians in the new Palestine.

LONDON, 1946

CHAPTER ONE

The Background

THERE IS A PASSAGE IN THE BIBLICAL BOOK OF ESTHER which might have been written by a twentieth century anti-Semite:

There is a certain people, scattered abroad and dispersed among the people in all the provinces of thy kingdom; and their laws are divers from all people; neither keep they the King's laws; therefore it is not for the King's profit to suffer them. If it please the King, let it be written that they may be destroyed.

In those words, placed in the mouth of Haman, the ancient book laid down the causes of Judophobia. A people dispersed, without a country of its own, yet refusing to disappear and retaining its own personality, provokes misunderstanding, fear and hostility. A direct line stretches from Haman to Hitler, from Haman's speech to the *Elders of Zion*. Such a historic phenomenon cannot be explained away by August Bebel's phrase, "Anti-Semitism is the Socialism of the fool." Despite the partial truth in this saying, it is still not clear why the fool's Socialism should take the form of anti-Semitism.

A people uprooted from its soil and scattered all over the globe would logically be expected to disappear in the course of a few generations. The Jewish people did not vanish, though large numbers of Jews left the community as a result of conversion, whether forced or voluntary, intermarriage or assimilation. There is hardly a nation in Europe without an admixture of Jewish blood. But the Jewish people itself has survived.

Even before the destruction of the second Jewish Commonwealth, the political conflict of the Jewish people with its enemies had a cultural and religious character. "Their laws are divers from all people." This was the history of the Maccabean struggle, this is behind the accusation of Tacitus:

. . . Moses gave a new form of worship, and a system of religious ceremonies, the reverse of everything known to any other age or country. Whatever is held sacred by the Romans, with the Jews is held profane; and what in other nations is unlawful and impure with them is fully established . . .

The Jews acknowledge one God only, and him they see in the mind's eye, and him they adore in contemplation, condemning as impious idolaters all who, with perishable materials wrought into the human form, attempt to give a representation of the Deity. The God of the Jews is the great governing mind that directs and guides the whole frame of nature, eternal, infinite and neither capable of change nor subject to decay. In consequence of this opinion no such thing as a statue was to be seen in their city, much less in their temples. Flattery had not learnt to pay that homage to their own kings, nor were they willing to admit the statues of the Caesars.

(Tacitus, *History,* Book V, Ch. 4-5)

The Talmud illustrates this ideological conflict by the following story:

The Emperor Hadrian said to Rabbi Joshua, son of Chananya: "I want to see your God." The Rabbi replied: "That is impossible." The Emperor said: "You must show Him to me." The Rabbi made the Emperor go outside with him. (It was summer, in the month of Tammuz.) He said to the Emperor: "Look at the sun." "I cannot," answered the Emperor. Then the Rabbi replied: "If you cannot even look at the sun, which is but one of the servants of the Holy One, blessed be He, how shall you look at the Holy One Himself?"

(Talmud Babli; *Chulin,* 59b, 60a)

The estrangement between Judaism and its offspring, Christianity, arose in the first century C.E., grew in subsequent centuries and developed into profound hostility. From the outset the Jews in the dispersion differed profoundly from their neighbors in their way of living, their religious, cultural and spiritual heritage. They had a definite individuality and an instinct of self-preservation which enabled them to resist the threat of destruction inherent in their position. They were determined to survive until redemption came.

It was against this background that Jewish-Gentile relations developed through the ages. The non-Jewish world, unable to digest the Jewish people, adopted — perhaps naturally — the policy of isolating them. And so the history of the Jewish people is one of persecution and suffering, with intervening periods of quiet and toleration, but never of real peace. Anti-Semitism found a thousand forms of expression: denial of civil rights, moral humiliation, religious persecution, economic isolation, exclusion from agriculture, restriction to money-lending and certain branches of commerce, segregation in ghettoes and pales of settlement, political discrimination, social ostracism, expulsion and physical annihilation. Throughout the entire history of the Diaspora there was hardly a moment when Jews were not being persecuted somewhere. An old Yiddish proverb says: When the sheep are sheared, the lambs shiver. Whenever Jews were persecuted in one land, Jews in other countries not only felt solidarity with the persecuted but were bound to reflect: Today it is happening there — who knows whether tomorrow it will not happen here. Thus, even during periods of relative quiet in any given country, the Jews were never able to forget the abnormality and instability of their position. A hundred years ago Heinrich Heine summed up this history in the bitterly ironic poem, *To Edom:*

The Background

Ein Jahrtausend schon und laenger
Dulden wir uns bruederlich;
Du, du duldest, dass ich atme,
Dass du rasest, dulde ich.

The Jewish people reacted like the man in the story of the sun and the wind; the more violent the storm, the more stubborn the resistance and the conviction that the only cure was the return to the ancient homeland.

ISRAEL ENTERS HISTORY

The earliest Hebrew connection with Palestine dates back almost four thousand years. According to Biblical tradition, Palestine became the *Land of Promise* before Abraham, the first ancestor of the nation, entered it at the end of the third, or the beginning of the second, millennium B.C. The covenant of the Lord with Abraham, promising the land of Canaan "to thee and thy seed . . . for an everlasting possession" (*Genesis* 17, 8), is connected with a warning of the Egyptian servitude which had to precede it. "Know of a surety that thy seed shall be a stranger in a land that is not theirs and shall serve them; and they shall afflict them four hundred years."

(*Gen.* 15, 13.)

It is as though at the threshold of its history the nation received the fateful warning: Palestine is indeed designated to serve as foundation for your life and development, but you must deserve it, and again and again show yourselves worthy of possessing it. Owning the land is not merely a right; it is a high responsibility. Again and again, in the Pentateuch and the Prophets, Israel is warned of the inevitable loss of Palestine in case of misbehavior. But this loss is never final; it is always only temporary. Always the proclamation of prospective exile is accompanied by the promise of return. No other nation can acquire a permanent right to the country. Constant struggle for the Land of Israel appears to be the basic law of Israel's history.

Hebrew tribes appear to have stayed in the country throughout the time when the children of Jacob sojourned in Egypt. The Exodus marked Israel's entrance into active history, and is still commemorated as such throughout the Jewish world. Passover is still celebrated as the "festival of our freedom." Changes may have taken place in its form but its content appears to have been altered very little in more than three thousand years. Whatever element of primitive spring festival it may have contained at its inception, has been overshadowed by the aspect of national redemption from Egyptian captivity. This has been true ever since the nation entered upon its historic curriculum. And it has remained so to this day, even though the very basis of the Passover festival might seem to have been destroyed by loss of independence and by dispersion. By persisting in its celebration of Passover as the festival of national freedom, the nation clearly signified that it did not accept dispersion as anything but temporary; that it regarded itself—dispersion and persecution notwithstanding—as the full heir of the freedom gained by the forefathers who had participated in the Exodus from Egypt.

"Slaves were we unto Pharaoh in Egypt"—so goes the explanation of the meaning of Passover on the evening of the festival—"and if the most Holy, blessed be He, had not brought forth our fathers from Egypt, we and our children and our children's children, had still continued in bondage to Pharaoh in Egypt . . ."

And: "In every generation each individual is bound to regard himself as if he had actually gone forth from Egypt . . . Not only our ancestors did the Holy One, blessed be He, redeem but us also did He redeem with them . . ."

Consistently enough, the narrative of the Exodus, recited on the night of Passover, is preceded by the expression of hope: "This year here, next year in the Land of Israel; this year slaves, next year free men," and concluded by the expression of yearning: "Next year in Jerusalem."

FROM CONQUEST TO CAPTIVITY

No exact dates can be fixed for the start and the completion of the conquest of Canaan by the Israelites. The differences of opinion among scholars concern a span of about two centuries. Professor John Garstang, for example, sets the "beginning of the history of Israel in Canaan under Joshua" at the end of the fifteenth century B.C. (*Joshua Judges,* London, 1931, p. 61); Sir Flinders Petrie considers the beginning of the twelfth century as the most probable date (*Egypt and Israel,* London, 1923, p. 53); while Sir George Adam Smith (*Historical Geography*) chooses the exact middle between the two extremes, around 1300 B.C. All, however, are agreed that the end of the era of foundation (the Judges) and the establishment of the monarchy under Saul took place before the end of the second millennium B.C. The height of Israel's power under David and Solomon comes to an end about 930 B.C. with the disruption of the kingdom into Israel in the North and Judah in the South. In 722 B.C. Israel's conquest by Sargon of Assyria resulted in the deportation of the ten northern tribes, who never reappeared in Jewish history. In 586 B.C. Judah was destroyed by Nebuchadnezzar and the aristocracy and a large part of the people were carried away into Babylonian captivity.

This is the bare skeleton of the first great epoch in Jewish history. We cannot deal here with the varied political and military fortunes of the nation, or the economic, social and religious development of its national life. We must confine ourselves to those aspects which left their mark on the fate of the Jewish people and its relationship to Palestine.

The Background

Sub specie eternitatis, this is the epoch of the great pre-exilic prophets of Israel: Elijah and Elisha, Amos, Hosea, Isaiah, Micah, Zephaniah, Nahum, Jeremiah; the epoch in which the foundation of Israel's religious and spiritual heritage to mankind was firmly laid. In this epoch Messianism—in all its aspects though not yet in name—was born.

Throughout its active history the Jewish people was conscious of its physical weakness as a small nation whose neighbors were mighty empires. If power alone were to decide the conflicts between nations, Israel had no prospect of survival. Only if justice were ultimately to prevail was there any hope. The very foundation of the nation was bound up with redemption by divine power from Egyptian bondage, and with divine intervention during the conquest of the land. Talmudic literature speaks of Moses as the first Redeemer and of the coming Messiah as the last. Stripped of all eschatological and supernatural elements, prophetic vision and messianic hope are the expression of a very realistic thesis: Israel's national security can be assured only in an atmosphere of international harmony and social justice. This ideal will be attained "in the last days" under Israel's leadership.

And many nations shall come, and say, Come, and let us go up to the mountain of the Lord, and to the House of the God of Jacob; and He will teach us of His ways, and we shall walk in His paths: for the law shall go forth of Zion, and the word of the Lord from Jerusalem.

And He shall judge among many people, and rebuke strong nations afar off; and they shall beat their swords into ploughshares, and their spears into pruning-hooks; nation shall not lift up sword against nation, neither shall they learn war any more.

(Micah, 4)

Peace among nations will be accompanied by social justice within the nations. "But with righteousness shall He judge the poor, and reprove with equity for the weak of the earth." And within this universal order Israel will be free and indeed acquire the moral leadership of the world:

And it shall come to pass in that day that the Lord shall set His hand again the second time to recover the remnants of His people . . . and He shall set up an ensign for the nations, and shall assemble the outcast of Israel, and gather together the depressed of Judah from the four corners of the earth.

CHAPTER TWO

From the First to the Second Commonwealth

THE PROPHECY OF THE INGATHERING OF THE EXILES was only partly fulfilled. The outcasts of Israel were never re-assembled after their expulsion in 722 B.C. The ten tribes suffered the fate of many other peoples and races in similar circumstances. They seem to have been submerged by their conquerors and so disappeared in the mists of history. If the southern part of the nation, conquered by Nebuchadnezzar in 586 B.C., had had the same fate, the entire history of mankind would have taken another turn. There would have been no Jewish problem, but neither would there have been Christianity.

Judah's reaction was different from Israel's. After the split into two kingdoms, Judah developed a high degree of religious and cultural individuality. The century and a half of its continued existence after the downfall of the

northern kingdom strengthened and deepened this process and endowed the people with the power to resist
physical submergence and cultural assimilation. This resistance is immortalized in songs of lament and prophecies
of hope, transmitted to posterity in the Bible.

By the rivers of Babylon, there we sat down, yea, we
wept, when we remembered Zion.
We hanged our harps upon the willows in the midst
thereof.
For there they that carried us away captive required of
us a song; and they that wasted us required of us mirth,
saying, Sing us one of the songs of Zion.
How shall we sing the Lord's song in a strange land?
If I forget thee, O Jerusalem, let my right hand forget
her cunning.
If I do not remember thee, let my tongue cleave to the
roof of my mouth; if I prefer not Jerusalem above my
chief joy.
Remember, O Lord, the children of Edom in the day
of Jerusalem; who said, Rase it, rase it, even to the
foundation thereof.
O daughter of Babylon, who are to be destroyed;
happy shall he be that rewardeth thee as thou hast
served us.
Happy shall he be, that taketh and dasheth thy little
ones against the stones.

(Psalm 137)

The curse of revenge was very soon to become reality.
A bare half century after Nebuchadnezzar's great military
triumphs, Babylon herself was conquered by Cyrus, the

26

founder of the Persian empire (538 B.C.). It was in anticipation of this historic event that Ezekiel, the prophet who was "among the captives by the river of Chebar," saw the vision "of the valley full of bones" which at the Lord's command "came together, bone to his bone . . . the sinews and the flesh came up upon them, and the skin covered them above . . . the breath came into them and they lived, and stood up upon their feet, an exceeding great army."

Then he said unto me, Son of man, these bones are the whole house of Israel. . . Behold, O my people, I will open your graves and cause you to come out of your graves and bring you into the land of Israel. . . And I shall put my spirit in you, and ye shall live, and I shall place you on your own land.

(Ezekiel, 37)

Ezekiel has good tidings not only for the people of Israel but also for the land which was bereaved of its people:

But ye, O mountains of Israel, ye shall shoot forth your branches, and yield your fruit to my people of Israel; for they are at hand to come.

For, behold, I am for you, and I will turn unto you, and ye shall be tilled and sown;

And I will multiply men upon you, all the House of Israel, even all of it: and the cities shall be inhabited, and the wastes shall be builded;

And I will multiply upon you man and beast: and they shall increase and bring fruit: and I will settle you

27

after your old estates, and will do better unto you than at your beginnings: and ye shall know that I am the Lord.

(Ezekiel 36:8-11)

THE CYRUS DECLARATION

The story of the restoration under Persian rule is so reminiscent of present-day events that it is worth recapitulating according to the records in *Ezra* and *Nehemiah*.

Now in the first year of Cyrus King of Persia . . . the Lord stirred up the spirit of Cyrus King of Persia, that he made a proclamation throughout all his kingdoms and put it also in writing, saying: Thus says Cyrus King of Persia, the Lord God of Heaven hath given me all the kingdoms of earth; and He hath charged me to build Him an house at Jerusalem, which is in Judah. Who is there among you of all His people? His God be with him and let him go up to Jerusalem, which is in Judah, and build the house of the Lord God of Israel (He is the God) which is in Jerusalem.

And 43,360 Jews, a comparatively large number for that time, set out for Palestine. Those who remained behind, "strengthened their hands with vessels of silver, with gold, with goods, and with beasts, and with precious things, besides all that was willingly offered." (Groups of re-emigrants followed at later dates, 458 under Ezra and 445 under Nehemiah.) The returning Jews expected no difficulties in the fulfillment of their task of resettlement and rebuilding. But in this they were mistaken. "The people of the land," consisting of foreign colonists, all of them adversaries of Judah and Benjamin, "weakened the hands of the people of Judah and troubled them in building, and hired counsellors against them to frustrate their purpose." They could hardly expect a recall of the Declaration or a denial of its existence, or an interpreting away of its meaning in Cyrus' lifetime. But no sooner was he dead than they began their political campaign for a change of policy. "Be it known unto the King (Artaxerxes) that the Jews which came up from thee to us are come unto Jerusalem, building the rebellious and the bad city . . . if this city be builded and the walls set up again, then they will not pay toll, tribute and custom . . . by this means thou shalt have no portion on this side of the river."

They got their wish, temporarily. Artaxerxes found "that this city of old time has made insurrections against kings, and that rebellion and sedition have been made therein." And he ordered "that this city be not builded, until another commandment shall be given from me."

But the Jews did not give in. Artaxerxes was followed by Darius, and in the second year of his reign (520 B.C.), inspired by the prophets Haggai and Zechariah, "rose up

Zerubbabel the son of Shealtiel, and Jeshua the son of Jozadak, and began to build the house of God which is at Jerusalem . . ."

The provocative question of their adversaries, "Who has commanded you to build this house and to make up this wall?" did "not cause them to cease, till the matter came to Darius: and then they returned answer by letter concerning this matter."

In their letter the Jews invoked both what we would now call "historical connection" and the promise made to them in the Cyrus Declaration.

We are the servants of the God of Heaven and earth, and build the house that was builded these many years ago, which a great king of Israel builded and set up. But after that our fathers had provoked the God of Heaven into wrath, He gave them into the hand of Nebuchadnezzar the King of Babylon, the Chaldean, who destroyed this house, and carried the people away into Babylon. But in the first year of Cyrus the King of Babylon the same King Cyrus made a decree to build this house of God.

(*Ezra,* 5:11-12)

Darius ordered a search to be made in the King's treasure house for the text of the Cyrus Declaration, which was found there. He then brushed aside the decree of Artaxerxes and restored the policy of Cyrus in letter and spirit. He commanded Tatnai, his "Governor beyond the river," and the whole administration thus: "Let the work of this house of God alone; let the Governor of the Jews and the elders of the Jews build this house of God in his place. Moreover, I make a decree what ye shall do to the elders of these Jews for the building of this house of God: that of the King's goods, even of the tribute beyond the river, forthwith expenses be given unto these men, that they be not hindered." Darius even proclaimed the death penalty for those who might still attempt to hamper the work, and called down the curse of God on them. And, to guard against possible administrative procrastination or sabotage, he concluded thus: "I Darius have made a decree; let it be done with speed."

The adversaries of the Jews did not confine themselves to purely political action. Sanballat, the Horonite, and Tobiah, the Ammonite, and Geshem, the Arabian, tried the method of direct action. Here is what Nehemiah tells us about his experiences while rebuilding the wall of Jerusalem in 445:

And all the wall was joined together unto the half thereof; for the people had a mind to work. But it came to pass that when Sanballat and Tobiah, and the Arabian, and the Ammonites, and the Ashdodites heard that the wall of Jerusalem was made up, and that the breaches began to be stopped, then they were very wroth. And conspired all of them together to come and to fight against Jerusalem, and to hinder it . . . And our adversaries said they shall not know, neither see, till we come in the midst amongst them, and slay them and cause the work to cease. . . .

(*Nehemiah*, 4)

31

But the Jews were not unaware of the danger. And they prepared to meet it.

And I (Nehemiah) looked and rose up and spake unto the nobles, and the rulers and to the rest of the people, Be not ye afraid of them: remember the Lord which is great and terrible, and fight for your brethren, your sons and your daughters, your wives and your houses. . . . And it came to pass from that time forth, that the half of my servants wrought in the work, and the other half of them held both the spears, the shields and the bows and the habergeons; and the rulers were behind all the house of Judah. They that builded on the wall, and they that bore burdens, with those that laded, every one with one of his hands wrought in the work and with the other hand held a weapon. For the builders every one had his sword girded by his side and so builded. . . . So neither I, nor my brethren, nor my servants, nor the men of the guard which followed me, none of us put off our clothes, saving that every one put them off for washing.

Does not history repeat itself?

CHAPTER THREE

The Struggle for Independence

RETURN FROM BABYLONIAN CAPTIVITY DID NOT IMPLY A restoration of Jewish independence. Judea remained a province of the Persian empire. With the Persian empire it fell to Alexander the Great, and after his death was for over a century the object of contention between the Egyptian Ptolemies and the Syrian Seleucides. Judea was "very like to a ship in a storm which is tossed by the waves on both sides" (Josephus, *Antiquities of the Jews,* XII, 3, 3). In 198 B.C. it was finally conquered by Syria.

Throughout those three centuries Judea enjoyed a considerable degree of internal freedom and autonomy. There was domestic trouble; there was strong, though peaceful, penetration of Hellenistic ideas, religious conceptions and customs. There was sharp conflict between Hellenizers and nationalists. But all that remained an internal affair so long as there was little interference from without. The beginning of the Seleucid regime seemed to promise a continuation of this state of affairs. Antiochus III (the Great) tried to win the friendship and confidence of the Jews by conceding them favorable treatment with regard to taxes and particularly by confirming their internal autonomy. "Let all of that nation live according to the laws of their own country" (Josephus, *Antiquities*, XII, 3, 3). But three decades later the drastic modification of this policy by his successor, Antiochus IV Epiphanes, provoked the rising of the Maccabees. The real significance of that event can only be understood if conceived as the beginning of an epoch which ended eight centuries later, with the Arab conquest (634-638 C.E.), and if this entire epoch is considered against the background of the general history of the civilized world of that time.

The victorious invasion of Asia by Alexander the Great was the first attempt at establishing the domination of the East by the West. Efforts in this direction continued after Alexander's death, and over a century later Rome took over the role of Macedonia. Rome's domination ultimately extended as far as the Euphrates, where it was checked first by the Parthians and later by their successors, the resurrected Persian kingdom. With the rise of Islam in the seventh century, the long epoch of Western domination over the East came to an end.

What was the place of the Jewish people in this historic struggle? The Maccabean War was not at first a struggle for complete independence. The Jewish people had learnt a very simple lesson from its history. Fate had placed it in a narrow geographical area, squeezed between competing great powers into whose conflicts it was inevitably dragged. In such a situation a policy of complete political isolation was impossible. The Jewish people had reconciled itself to this fate and was prepared to become part of a larger political unit provided only that it was allowed to live its life in its own way. So long as the dominating power—Persia, Alexander's empire, Egypt (the Greeks of the South), Syria (the Greeks of the north)—confined itself to political suzerainty without interfering in the internal life of the nation, the Jews gave little trouble. The trouble began when these essentials were attacked. And this Antiochus Epiphanes did; was bound to do.

When the Seleucid Empire definitely established its rule over Palestine in 198 B.C., it was already an empire in decline. Rome had just rounded off its domination over the western part of the Mediterranean area by the victorious conclusion of the second Punic War. Now it began to look to the East and immediately came into collision with Syria. In 190 B.C. Syria suffered a crushing defeat in the battle of Magnesia and was driven out of Greece and Asia Minor. "With the day of Magnesia, Asia (Syria) was erased from the list of great states" (Mommsen, *History of Rome,* III, 9). In 168, Antiochus IV Epiphanes was ordered by Rome to evacuate Egypt which he had successfully invaded. Not only were Syria's expansionist ambitions checked in the West, but some of the countries in the East, where Rome did not yet challenge Syria's rule, began to fall away. Under the impact of this state of affairs Antiochus Epiphanes tried to save what re-

mained of his empire by strengthening its internal cohesion. He aimed at the fusion of all the divergent races
of the empire into one people by the introduction of
Greek religion and culture as a uniting factor for all sec-
tions of its population.

. . . King Antiochus wrote to his whole kingdom that
all should be one people. And everyone should leave his
laws. . . .

(I Maccabees, I, 41-42)

For the Jews he issued the most detailed orders. He
prohibited offerings in the Temple, observance of the
Sabbath and circumcision, and ordered the pollution of
the Temple, the erection of chapels and altars for idols,
and the sacrifice of swine's flesh, "to the end that they
might forget the law and change all the ordinances." Any
transgression was punishable by death, and overseers were
sent everywhere to enforce the orders. Conflict with the
Jewish people thus became inevitable.

Passive resistance turned into active insurrection when
the King's overseers reached the town of Modein, the
home of Mattathias of the house of Hasmon. He was
called on, as "a ruler and an honorable and great man
in this city," to be the first to "fulfil the King's commandment, like as all the heathen have done, yea and the men
of Judah also, and such as remain in Jerusalem."

Then Mattathias answered and spake with a loud voice:
Though all the nations that are under the King's do-

36

minion obey him, and fall away every one from the religion of their fathers, and give consent to his commandments; yet will I and my sons and my brethren walk in the covenant of our fathers. God forbid that we should forsake the Law and the ordinances. We will not hearken to the King's words to go from our religion, either on the right hand, or on the left.

This was the signal for open rebellion.

ENTER ROME AND PARTHIA

The Maccabean struggle against Syria lasted almost forty years, until 129 B.C., when Judea won its full independence. But, characteristically enough, in the memory of the nation this struggle has been immortalized by the festival of "Hanukah," instituted by Judas Maccabeus, the chief leader of the rebellion, in 165, as a memorial of the purification of the Temple and its rededication to the worship of the God of Israel. All that followed was overshadowed in the memory of the people by the one great historic fact: that by the people's heroic resistance led by God's fatherly grace, the heritage of their forefathers, their religion and culture, was saved from submergence in the sea of Hellenistic civilization.

The struggle had to go on even after the conclusion in

163 of a peace by which the new king, Antiochus V Eupator, formally abandoned the policy of his predecessors and conceded to the Jews "that they shall walk after their own laws, as aforetime." (*I Maccabees,* VI 59-61)

The treacherous demolition of the fortress of Mount Zion as soon as peace was concluded, showed the Jews that their internal liberty could never be safe so long as they remained under Seleucid overlordship. In the course of its struggle, Judea for the first time came into contact with the two powers whose rivalry was to become the outstanding factor in world history for centuries—Rome and Parthia.

After the battle of Magnesia the power of Rome had become dominant in the countries of the Eastern Mediterranean and Western Asia. The way in which Egypt was delivered from Syrian conquest by the order of Rome could not have remained unknown to the Jewish leaders. Many other countries, such as Numidia, Pergamus, Bithynia, Cappadocia, even Syria herself, had to seek safety in alliances with Rome which implied the recognition, in one way or another, of Rome's superiority. It was therefore in accordance with the world situation at the time that Judas Maccabeus applied for an alliance with Rome. Rome and Judea had a common object: to weaken Syria's power. It is true that Rome's promise of active help, "if war come first upon the nation of the Jews," did not in fact result in any active Roman intervention. Still, the pact of friendship was of importance to the Jews, if only because it implied political and diplomatic recognition of their land as an entity separate from Syria—perhaps a first step to independence.

At the same time the Parthians entered Jewish history. They had shaken off the Syrian yoke about 250 B.C. They emerged as a great power in the middle of the second century B.C., thus introducing "that gradual waning of the Syrian and advance of the Parthian state, which is the chief fact of West Asian history in the two centuries immediately preceding our era." (*Parthia,* by George Rawlinson, London, 1894, p. 62)

There was a conspicuous similarity between Parthian and Jewish resistance to Hellenization.

The Parthian kingdom was thoroughly anti-Hellenic. It appealed to patriotic feelings, and to the hate universally felt towards the stranger. It set itself to undo the work of Alexander, to cast out the Europeans, to recover for the native race the possession of its own continent. "Asia for the Asiatics" was its cry.

(*Parthia, op. cit.* p. 47)

And Mommsen:

Since the days of Alexander the world had obeyed the Occidentals alone. . . With Mithridates I the East re-entered the sphere of political movement. The world had again two masters.

(*History of Rome,* Book IV, I)

It was just at the time of the Maccabean war that Syria had to turn her attention to this new and dangerous rival. Almost simultaneously with the attack on the Jews,

Antiochus Epiphanes marched into Persia (Parthia) to enforce the payment of tribute by the Eastern provinces and to ransack the temples of Ahuramazda and Mithra as he had ransacked that of Jerusalem.

Just as in Judea—only with a wider range and ampler proportions—the result was a reaction on the part of the native religion against Hellenism and the Hellenic gods; the promoters of this movement were the Parthians, and out of it arose the great Parthian Empire.

(*Mommsen,* Book IV, I)

Antiochus was thus compelled to divide his forces, a fact which greatly contributed to Judas Maccabeus' victory over the reduced Syrian armies. The news of this defeat reached Antiochus Epiphanes just after his own disaster in the battle of Elymais in Persia.

In 129 B.C. it was the crushing defeat of Antiochus Sidetes by the Parthians which made it possible for John Hyrkanos to put an end to Judea's vassal relation with Syria and to restore the full independence of the country. Parthia's rise as the Empire of the East, and Judea's advance to independence thus not only coincide in time, but are in fact interconnected. The Parthia-Rome jealousy had not yet arisen.

The Struggle for Independence

After sixty-five years of independence—and even substantial military successes and extension of territory—Judea fell victim in 63 B.C. to the conquering march of Rome in the East, as Pontus, Armenia and other small and large nations, once vassals of Syria, and Syria herself.

Parthia alone successfully resisted Rome's attempts at subjugation. In a long struggle, during which she experienced varying fortunes, Parthia not only retained her independence but became a challenging rival of Rome. This rivalry continued even after the Parthian, Arsacides, had been replaced by the Persian, Sassanides, and the place of the Roman Empire had been taken by Byzantium. It ended only with the rise of Mohammedan power in the seventh century of the present era.

At first Judea was not simply incorporated into the Roman State. Rome remained "faithful" to the pact of friendship dating from the days of Judas Maccabeus and repeatedly confirmed in later years; this pact, the argument seems to have been, while not guaranteeing Judea full independence, did safeguard the internal autonomy which she had enjoyed before Antiochus Epiphanes' attack. As the lawful heir of Syria, Rome simply restored the "status quo," abolished the Jewish kingdom and installed Hyrkanos, one of two brothers fighting for the throne, as ruling high priest, thus reducing Judea to the status of a vassal. Even Josephus described the real situation in the plain words: "For now we lost our liberty, and became subject to the Romans." (*Antiquities* XIII, IV, 5)

Again, as in the days of the Maccabees, this small people presented its conqueror with an unprecedented problem. It was quite unlike the other peoples, who, however stubborn and cruel the struggle, fitted themselves into the new framework with more or less ease, as soon as they realized that they were beaten. In the case of the Jews, it was not a simple fight between a weak and a strong people; it was a clash between two worlds, each without a key to the understanding or appreciation of the other.

The nature of this conflict between Judaism and paganism was clearly understood by Roman writers.

As early as 58 B.C. Cicero, in his oration in defence of L. Flaccus, exclaimed that "the religious ceremonies and observances of that people (the Jews) are very much at variance with the splendor of this Empire, the dignity of our name, and the institutions of our ancestors." (*The Orations of Marcus Tullius Cicero,* Bohn's Classical Library, Vol. II, p. 454)

Tacitus (*see above, p.* 17), who wrote at the end of the first century C.E., rightly regards the clash between Rome and Judea as a continuation of the struggle of Maccabean days. He feels a very close affinity of mind and sympathy with Antiochus Epiphanes, who formed a plan to weed out the superstition of the country (Judea). To reform, if possible, so corrupt a race, he intended to introduce the manners and institutions of Greece; but a war with the Parthians (Arsaces being then in arms) rendered that design abortive. (*Op. cit.,* Chap. VIII)

And Dio Cassius in 230 C.E.—

They are distinguished from the rest of mankind in practically every detail of life, and especially by the fact that they do not honor any of the usual gods, but show extreme reverence for one particular divinity. They never had any statue of him even in Jerusalem itself, but believing him to be unnamable and invisible, they worship him in the most extravagant fashion on earth. (*Roman History,* translated by Earnest Cary. The Loeb Classical Library, New York. Volume III, Book XXXXVII 17, 2)

The 130 years between Pompey's subjugation of Judea and the destruction of the Temple were a period of permanent friction and revolt. Mommsen (Book V, Ch. IV) speaks of the "obstinate resistance which the tough Jewish nation opposed to the conqueror." Between 57 and 54 B.C. three separate revolts against the "unnatural yoke" broke out which Gabinus, Roman Governor of Syria, had great difficulty in suppressing. "In consequence of this even the monarchy of the high priest was abolished. The Jewish land was broken up . . . into five independent districts administered by governing colleges." (Mommsen, l.c.). Hyrkanos thus lost his secular powers and was restricted to purely priestly functions.

These happenings again were connected with the tense relations between Rome and Parthia, which culminated in war between them. In 53 B.C. Crassus was defeated by the Parthians at Carrhae and lost his life. In 52 B.C. the Jews again rose, but were subdued by Cassius with the help of the Idumean Herodes Antipater, the minister of the high priest, Hyrkanos. In 47 B.C., Julius Caesar restored Hyrkanos to his secular rights and even returned Joppa to the Jewish vassal state. The actual ruler, however, was Antipater. "Thus under the name of the Hasmonean prince, a half foreigner governed the Jewish state under the protection and according to the will of Rome. The Jews with national sentiments were anything but inclined towards the new government." (Mommsen, *Provinces,* Book VIII, Ch. XI, p. 176)

After Caesar's death the Parthians again overran Asia Minor and Syria, and invaded Palestine (40 B.C.). "The (Hasmonean) Pretender Antigonus joined them, and possessed himself of Jerusalem and almost the whole territory." (Mommsen, 1.c., p. 177.) For four years Hasmonean rule was restored. But with the withdrawal of the Parthians, Herod, with Roman support, reconquered the country and ruled it as a Roman vassal until his death in 4 C.E. It was an unhappy, bloodstained reign, never really accepted by the people. After Herod's death Jewish independence was entirely nullified. Judea proper was taken under direct Roman administration, Galilee made into a "tetrarchy" under the Herodians, which subsisted down to the time of Trajan.

The struggle was not purely political. The reason for one insurrection towards the close of Herod's life was the introduction of a golden eagle into the Temple, magnificently rebuilt by him.

Much as they admired the building, his introduction into it of a golden eagle was taken more amiss than all the sentences of death ordained by him and led to a popular insurrection to which the eagle fell a sacrifice, and thereupon doubtless the devotees as well who tore it down.
                                        (*Mommsen*, l.c., p. 181)

Once again, in the year 40 C.E., the Jews defied the command of the Emperor Caligula to place his statue in the Temple, a command accentuated by the dispatch to the country of an army under Petronius with instructions "that in case the Jews would not admit of them, he should slay those that opposed it and carry all the rest of the nation into captivity." (Josephus, *Wars of the Jews,* Book II, Ch. X.) Like the emissaries of Antiochus Epiphanes two centuries before, Petronius argued with the Jews that "their petition [for the revocation of the order] was unreasonable, because while all the nations in subjection to them had placed the images of Caesar in their several cities, among the rest of their gods, for them alone to oppose it was almost like the behavior of revolters and was injurious to Caesar." This argument was reinforced by invoking "the power of the Romans and the threatenings of Caesar."

Again, in a manner which in the new circumstances showed no less courage than Mattathias had displayed in his time, the Jews answered "That if he would place the images among them, he must first sacrifice the whole Jewish nation; and that they were ready to expose themselves together with their children and wives to be slain." Petronius "was astonished, and pitied them on account of the inexpressible sense of religion the men were under and that courage of theirs, which made them ready to die for it," and decided to recommend to Caligula the withdrawal of the order, knowing that he might pay for this disobedience with his life. Caligula did, in fact, threaten to put him to death. The outbreak of the final armed clash was postponed by two decades by the sudden death of Caius Caligula.

The religious degradation of the world was such that not a protest was raised against the sacrileges of the Caesar; each worship was eager to ascribe to him the titles and honors which it reserved for its gods. It is to the eternal glory of the Jews that, amid all this base idolatry, they uttered the cry of conscientious indignation. Alone affirming that their religion was the absolute religion, they did not bend to the hateful caprice of the tyrant.

(Renan, *The Apostles,* Chap. XI)

But the clash was inevitable. One Roman Procurator after another provoked the Jewish people by trampling on their religious feelings, profaning the Temple, robbing its treasury and imposing intolerable taxation. The people

46

retorted by revolt after revolt. In the year 66 the rebellion developed into a serious war.

THE SECOND DESTRUCTION

It took the mighty Roman Empire almost seven years to break the last resistance of the tiny nation which, moreover, was lamentably divided into factions relentlessly fighting one another. The defeat of the Roman army under Cestius Gallus, the stubborn defence of the fortress Jotapata in Galilee, the desperate struggle for Jerusalem and the Temple, the holding out of the mountain fortress of Masada for three years after the fall of Jerusalem, bear witness to a spirit of courage and defiance outstanding in the history of the fight for freedom.

Even Tacitus could not help writing about the siege of Jerusalem:

There were weapons for all that could carry them; and more than could be expected, for their number, were bold enough to do so. The men and women were equally obstinate; and when they supposed they were carried away captive they were more afraid of life than of death.
(*History*, V, 13)

Josephus, commandant of Jotapata, according to his

own report, showed signs of defeatism and lack of courage even during the defence, and after the fall of the fortress cravenly delivered himself to the Romans' mercy. By saving his own life, however, he saved from oblivion a great and tragic epoch of Jewish history. In what amounts to a terrible self-indictment, he quotes his surviving comrades admonishing him to die rather than yield to the enemy:

. . . God has created the souls of the Jews of such a temper that they despise death . . . Canst thou bear to see the light in a state of slavery? . . . We ought to take care that the glory of our forefathers may not be tarnished. We will lend thee our right hand and a sword; and if thou wilt die willingly, thou wilt die as general of the Jews; but if unwillingly, thou wilt die as a traitor to them.

(Wars of the Jews, VIII, 4)

They decided to kill one another, "for they thought death, if Josephus might but die with them, was sweeter than life." But Josephus did not, after all, follow them into death . . .

And now the last act of the tragedy, the speeches of Eleazar, commandant of Masada, on the eve of the fortress' capture by the Romans:

Since we, long ago, my generous friends, resolved never to be servants to the Romans nor to any other than to God Himself, who alone is the true and just Lord of mankind, the time is now come that obliges us to make that resolution true in practice . . .

The Struggle for Independence

I cannot but esteem it a favor that God hath granted us, that it is still in our power to die bravely, and in a state of freedom, which hath not been the case of others who were conquered unexpectedly . . . Let our wives die before they are abused, and our children before they have tasted of slavery, and after we have slain them let us bestow that glorious benefit upon one another mutually and preserve ourselves in freedom, as an excellent funeral monument for us. But first let us destroy our money and the fortress by fire . . . and let us spare nothing but our provisions; for they will be a testimony when we are dead that we were not subdued for want of necessaries but that, according to our original resolution, we have preferred death before slavery.

When some of his comrades still hesitated, because of their wives and children, Eleazar appealed to their belief in the immortality of the soul and in the life to come:

How absurd a thing it is to pursue after liberty while we are alive and yet to envy it to ourselves where it will be eternal. We, therefore, who have been brought up in a discipline of our own ought to become an example to others of our readiness to die. . . . And as for those who are already dead, it is reasonable we should esteem them blessed, for they are dead in defending and not in betraying their liberty; but as to the multitude of those that are now under the Romans, who would not pity their condition? And who would not make haste to die before he would suffer the same miseries with them? . . . And where is now that great city, the metropolis of the Jewish nation? . . . Where is the city that was believed to have

God Himself inhabiting therein? . . .

Now who is there that resolves these things in his mind and yet is able to bear the sight of the sun? . . . Let us die before we become slaves of our enemies and let us go out of the world, together with our children and our wives, in a state of freedom. . . .

The Romans found a fortress of the dead. A chapter of the story of *Kiddush Hashem* (the martyr's sanctification of the Name of the Lord) had been written.

Rome had triumphed. Titus' victory procession in the capital of the Empire was adorned with captive leaders of the revolt. To this day every history text book shows the coin of commemoration, "Judea capta" (captured Judea). The Arch of Titus, with reliefs of Jewish captives and of treasures looted from the Temple, still stands on the bank of the Tiber in Rome.

CHAPTER FOUR

Resistance Continues

IT IS POPULARLY BELIEVED — BY NON-JEWS AND JEWS
alike — that the fall of Jerusalem and the destruction
of the Temple in 70 C.E., represent the last act in the great
drama of the Jewish people's history on its own soil, or,
at the very latest, the crushing of Bar Cochba's revolt in
the year 135. From this assumption far-reaching and
often unfounded conclusions are drawn concerning the
historical connection of the Jewish people with the Land
of Israel.

The second destruction undoubtedly marked a most
dangerous crisis in the life of the nation. The last remnant
of political independence had been lost. Hundreds of
thousands had died in battle. Thousands of young people
who found themselves still alive at the end of the war
perished in combat with wild beasts in the gladiatorial
arena for the victor's entertainment. Thousands were sold
into slavery. Others fled to neighboring countries. As the

51

Jewish peasant was the principal bearer of the Jewish revolt, Vespasian set about to destroy this class of the population primarily. He declared the whole of the land his property and ordered it to be sold and settled by Roman soldiers. The object was to change the character of the country entirely. Strict precautions were taken to prevent the rebuilding of the Temple, in the anticipation that with its disappearance the spiritual cohesion between the scattered parts of the nation would vanish, and even the nucleus in Palestine would become just one more of the many insignificant religious sects whose existence could in no way interfere with Roman world domination.

The Jewish people clearly understood what had happened.

Ye husbandmen, sow not again;
And thou, earth, wherefore givest thou the fruits of thy
     produce?
Keep within thee the sweets of thy sustenance.
And thou, vine, why further dost thou give thy wine?
For an offering shall not again be made therefrom in
     Zion.
Nor shall first-fruits again be offered.
And do ye, O heavens, withhold your dew,
And open not the treasuries of rain;
And do thou, O sun, withhold the light of thy rays;
And do thou, O moon, extinguish the multitude of thy
     light;
For why should light rise again
Where the light of Zion is darkened?

And you, ye bridegrooms, enter not in.
And let not the brides adorn themselves with garlands;
And, ye women, pray not that ye may bear,
For the barren shall rejoice more,
And those who have no sons shall be glad,
And those who have sons shall have anguish.
For why should they bear in pain
Only to bury in grief?
Or wherefore, again, should mankind have sons;
Or wherefore should the seed of their nature again be
    named,
Where this mother is desolate,
And her sons are led into captivity?
From this time forward speak not of beauty,
And discourse not of gracefulness.
Moreover, ye priests, take ye the keys of the sanctuary,
And cast them into the height of heaven,
And give them to the Lord, and say:
Guard Thy house Thyself,
For lo, we are found false stewards.

> (*Apocalypse of Baruch*, written at the
> end of the first century C.E.)*

But this was not the end by far.

It is one of the curiosities of Jewish history that the treachery of a Jewish prince who had fought his own people at the side of the Romans—Agrippa II, King of

---

The Apocrypha and Psuedo-epigrapha of the Old Testament, Ed.
R. H. Charles, D.Litt., D.D., Clarendon Press, Oxford, 1913. Vol. II,
pp. 485/6.

Galilee—saved his kingdom, and thereby provided a free haven for thousands of refugees from Judea. This fact had important results for centuries afterwards.

. . . Judea proper, though depopulated and impoverished, remained still Jewish as before; the light in which the (Roman) government looked upon the land is shown by the thoroughly anomalous permanent military occupation, which, as Judea was not situated on the frontier of the empire, can only have been destined to keep down the inhabitants.

(Mommsen, *History of Rome: The Provinces,* Vol. II, p. 218)

The Jewish people did not confine itself to lamentation; nor did it console itself merely by exalted hopes of messianic redemption in a more or less distant future. It acted, with an elasticity and adaptability to new circumstances which thwarted all the conqueror's anticipations.

Active measures were taken to retain the Jewish character of Palestine. Many who had fled from Roman vengeance returned. Residence in *Eretz Israel* was declared an act of great religious merit, and departure from the country, except under specified circumstances, highly reprehensible.

It was not a simple matter to achieve the planned displacement of Jewish peasants on a large scale by confiscating and selling their land. There seems to have been a shortage of Romans and other Gentiles in Palestine who were eager for this transaction, and the importation of such people in large numbers would not have been easy. The system was turned into a source of speculation for would-be colonists, who made large profits from the Jews' anxiety to repurchase their own land. The Rabbis ruled that a purchase of this character might be transacted even on the Sabbath. Other exemptions from Jewish canon law were also sanctioned, "for the sake of the resettlement of the land." As a result, after a number of years the Jewish population of Palestine was still mainly agricultural, and the agriculture of the country was still mainly Jewish.

Vespasian made what he evidently considered to be a gesture of political wisdom when he consented to Rabbi Jochanan Ben-Zakkai's plea, "Give me Jabne and its scholars." Jabne was transformed by the Jewish people into a new center for the Jews in Palestine and for the entire Diaspora. It took the place of Jerusalem; the Synagogue replaced the Temple; prayer replaced sacrifice. The function of the priest had been rendered impossible, but the authority of the teacher of the Law (Rabbi) was extended and strengthened. The Sanhedrin was reestablished in Jabne, with functions revised to suit the new conditions. It became a religious academy for the study and interpretation of the Law, and more than that, the religious legislative and judicial authority. Its rulings were accepted by Jewry throughout the world, and its head— the Nassi or Patriarch — was soon recognized as the spokesman of the Jewish people both in Palestine and abroad. The effect of Vespasian's callous decree converting the annual tax formerly paid by the Jews of the

Diaspora to the Temple in Jerusalem into a tax for the temple of Jupiter Capitolinus in Rome was neutralized by the Jews who created a new voluntary tax for the benefit of the Sanhedrin.

That the sums flowing into Palestine by this means must have been very considerable is evident from the eagerness of the Roman conquerors to get hold of them. Even before Vespasian, at least one Roman provincial administrator is known to have confiscated for the benefit of the Roman treasury the money destined for Palestine. This is what Cicero says in his oration *Pro Flacco* (1st century B.C.):

As gold, under pretence of being given to the Jews, was accustomed every year to be exported out of Italy and all the provinces to Jerusalem, Flaccus issued an edict establishing a law that it should not be lawful for gold to be exported out of Asia.

He goes on to enumerate the amounts of gold seized and sent to Rome: about a hundred pounds in Apamea, twenty in Laodicea, and smaller quantities in Addramythium and Pergamus. Later in the same century, Josephus relates, the Greeks of Libya laid hands on the "sacred money" of the Jews, and the Emperor Augustus ordered that the Jews' "sacred money be not touched but be sent to Jerusalem." Similar orders were issued to other provinces.

Four and a half centuries later, in 399 C.E., Honorius, ruler of the Western Roman Empire, forbade the payment of contributions to the Patriarch and ordered that the sums collected be turned over to the Imperial treasury. In the Eastern Empire, after the termination of the Patriarchate, all Jews were ordered to pay their regular contributions to the Imperial treasury.

For three and a half centuries, however, the Sanhedrin and the Patriarchate existed as the central authorities of the Jews of the Roman Empire. For three and a half centuries after the destruction of Jerusalem, Rome—pagan and after 312, Christian—still recognized Palestine as the center and focus of the Jewish people.

WAR AGAIN

Meanwhile, under the ashes the spark of insurrection still glowed, awaiting the opportunity to leap into flame. The first real conflagration broke out in 115 C.E., when the Roman Empire was engaged in a perilous struggle against a powerful combination of Eastern countries which the Emperor Trajan, imitating Alexander, had tried to subjugate.

Now the Jews thought their chance had arrived. In every quarter of the world, in each of their great settlements in Babylonia, Egypt and Cyrene, and in Judea, during the sovereignty of Trajan and his successor, the

57

Jews broke out into bold and open rebellion—not without considerable successes—and were finally subdued, only after an obstinate struggle and enormous loss of life.

(Millman, *History of the Jews*)

Mommsen, by no means prejudiced in favor of the Jews, wrote in his *Roman History:*

If the successes of this Emperor [Trajan] melted away under his hands at the end of his career, the Jewish insurrection, especially in Palestine and Mesopotamia, had its share in it.

(*The Provinces,* Vol. II, p. 222)

In 132 the revolt broke out again, with a violence unsurpassed even in the war against Vespasian. The cause was again the conqueror's failure to understand the individuality of the vanquished and the intensity of their national religious life. To Hadrian, the Jews—like other conquered peoples—were objects of the victor's will, with no say in their own fate, who could only hope for the master's good will and benevolence. There was no need to understand and respect their mentality; one and the same set of rules could be applied to all of them mechanically. One of Hadrian's predecessors had prohibited castration throughout the empire. Circumcision was reminiscent of castration—it must therefore be forbidden. Hadrian had a passion for rebuilding ruined cities and adorning them with magnificent temples. Jerusalem lay destroyed, the Temple in ashes. Surely the Jews would be delighted if their city were rebuilt, repopulated as a

Roman colony with a splendid temple — dedicated to Jupiter Capitolinus, of course. Such, at any rate, would have been the reaction of some of the multitude of conquered peoples who lived under the shadow of Rome. Not so the Jews. In the words of the Roman historian Dio Cassius, they were "sore angered that aliens should be settled in their own city and that foreign rites should be established in it."

And so, as Dio Cassius has it, "a war was kindled, no small one, nor short-lived." The insurrection was led by Bar-Cochba and, according to Mommsen, "had not its match in the history of the Roman imperial period." The Jewish world was stirred to its depths. Thousands hastened to Palestine from Egypt, Mesopotamia, Cyrene and other countries, to take part in the fighting. Soon a large part of the country, including the capital, was in Bar-Cochba's hands. "Deliverance of Jerusalem" was struck across the face of the coins of Titus, as a symbol of the liquidation of the Roman conquest. For over three years the Jews withstood the onslaught of the Roman legions. Julius Severus, Hadrian's greatest general, had to be recalled from Britain to save the prestige of the empire. His ultimate victory was achieved not in general battle but in piecemeal engagements and blockades. Dio Cassius says:

Of their forts, the fifty strongest were razed to the ground. Nine hundred and eighty-five of their best-known villages were destroyed. Fifty-eight myriads of men were slaughtered in skirmish and battle. Of those who perished of famine and disease there is no one can count the number. . .

And he adds significantly:

Many also of the Romans were slain in the war. Wherefore Hadrian, writing to the Senate, would not use the Emperor's wonted opening form of words, "I and the army are well."

No wonder that the Senate voted a monument to him "for his deliverance of the Empire from a redoubtable enemy," and that Julius Severus was awarded the ornaments of triumph "for the good finish of the affairs of the Jews."

The victor's vengeance was frightful. Its object was not to punish, nor disarm the vanquished, but to annihilate them physically and mentally. Most of the population of Judea was exterminated, the province itself laid in ruins. Those who had not died by the sword, by famine or pestilence were sold into slavery by the thousands. On the ruins of Jerusalem a new city was built, as planned by Hadrian before the war. It was named Aelia Capitolina and Jews were banned from it on pain of death. Only once a year, on the ninth day of Ab, anniversary of the destruction, were they allowed to approach the place where the Temple had stood and to lament its passing.*

---

*This ban on entering Jerusalem continued practically down to the Arab conquest. St. Jerome wrote about it in the 4th century: "The traitorous inhabitants are forbidden access to Jerusalem even to this

The very name of the country was changed to Syria Palestina. But this was not yet all. Hadrian had learned his lesson and did not want to repeat Vespasian's mistake. To make an end of the Jewish trouble once and for all, something more radical had to be done.

Jewish religious practice was forbidden, not circumcision only, but even the teaching of the Law. The long roll of Jewish martyrdom accords a place of honor to the "ten murdered by the State" — ten Rabbis, including Akiba, who were put to death for defying the ban. Religious persecution was so fierce that, to preserve the physical existence of the people, the Rabbinical Assembly allowed certain transgressions of the Law with the absolute exceptions of adultery, active idolatry and murder.

The nation never fully recovered from these terrible blows. It had moved a fateful step further in the process of losing grip on the country. Yet it did not give up.

---

day. With gold they have to purchase the indulgence to lament the destruction of their state. They who once shed the blood of Christ have now actually to pay for their tears. There, where on the summit of the Mount of Olives is the emblem of the Cross, we see a people, pitiful yet not to be pitied, weeping for the ruin of their temple. While their eyes are yet full of tears, the watchman demands from them the fee for permission to shed more tears."

THREE LINES OF DEFENSE

The war of Bar-Cochba had been fought mainly in Judea, which lay waste at the end of it. Galilee had suffered much less. Large numbers of refugees from Judea again found a haven in Galilee, whither the central national institutions — Sanhedrin and Patriarchate — were also transferred. "That latter country above all received a new impulse from the emigration, and for centuries afterwards remained an almost exclusively Jewish country." (Ernest Renan, *The History of the Origins of Christianity,* Book VI, p. 127)

George Adam Smith speaks of the Galilee of those centuries as "the sanctuary of the race and the home of their theological schools." (*Historical Geography of the Holy Land,* 20th edition, p. 425)

But about half a century following the Bar-Cochba disaster a revival of Judea began, though it never again became "an almost exclusively Jewish country." No fewer than about 400 villages and small towns are mentioned in the Jerusalem Talmud and in Midrashic literature as having a Jewish population at that period.

There is ample historical proof that the Jewish population still lived mainly by agriculture. The Jerusalem Talmud, which was completed about the end of the fourth century C.E., devotes ten of its sixty-five tractates to agricultural life and religious problems connected with it: land tenure, harvest, *shemitah* (the agricultural Sabbatical year), tithes, first-fruit offerings, etc. In the third century the Jewish religious authorities relaxed the ordinances about the *shemitah* year to make it possible for the Jews to pay the heavy taxes imposed by the conqueror. This measure, like the relaxation of the Law mentioned above, was intended to strengthen the Jewish hold upon the soil of the country.

Towards the end of the fourth century Rabbi Johanan, a Babylonian Tanaite who had returned to Palestine, said that "the major part of Eretz-Israel is in the hand of Israel."* In the *Life of Barsauma* it is stated that this brigand monk who visited Palestine about 400 C.E. suffered persecution, "for there were few Christians in Palestine, and the Jews and Samaritans who dominated the country persecuted them."†

The following two centuries saw a steady decline of the Jewish population. On the eve of the Arab invasion, the Christians—strengthened no doubt by large numbers of Jewish converts—formed the majority in the country. But the fact that the Jews were still in a position to raise an

---

*Quoted from the Jerusalem Talmud in Rabbi J. L. Fishman's *Religious Zionism and its Development* (Hebrew), Jerusalem, 1937, p. 119

†Quoted by James Parkes, *The Conflict of the Church and the Synagogue*, London, 1934, p. 233, from F. Nau's "Life of Barsauma" in *Revue de l'Orient Chrétien*, 1913

army of 20,000 (according to Eutyches*) or even 26,000 (according to Gibbon†) shows that they must still have numbered some hundreds of thousands. Their main strength appears to have been centered in Galilee, although there were Jews in other parts of the country. In the extreme south, in Macna on the shores of the Gulf of Akaba, in Adzruh and Jarba (northeast of the Gulf), Mahomet found independent Jewish communities, "At the same time [630 C.E.] deputations from Jewish settlements at Macna, Adzruh, and Jarba presented themselves with a tender of submission to the Prophet [at Tebuk]. To each was given a rescript, specifying the amount of their tribute, and binding them to afford refuge and aid to any Moslem travellers or merchants who might stand in need of their good offices."‡

Until the sixth century there existed on the island of Tiran (Jotaba), at the southern end of the Gulf of Akaba, an independent Jewish tribe which Justinian subjected. The Jewish population in the south of the country was strengthened, just before the Arab invasion, by the Jewish tribes of Beni-Canucaa and Beni-Nadhir, who, after being defeated (624-5) and expelled from Arabia by Mahomet, settled around Adraat in Transjordan and

---

Eutychii Annales, Palestine Pilgrim's Text Society, vol. XI, p. 36
†*Decline and Fall of the Roman Empire,* Chapter 50
‡ Sir William Muir, *The Life of Mahomet,* 3rd Edition, London, 1894, p. 429. The passage quoted is based on the Arab historian Wakidy's 8th century *Kitab al Maghazi*

in Jericho.*

Agricultural settlement was one line of defense. The second was in the spiritual and cultural field, what may be called the Jabne line. The place of Jabne in desolate Judea was taken successively by Usha, Shefaram, Beth-Shearim, Sephoris, and finally by Tiberias, which "became for several centuries the central point of Jewish learning" (Robinson, *Biblical Researches,* III, p. 269). The authority of the Patriarchate was strengthened. "The Patriarchs enjoyed almost royal authority. Their functions were political rather than religious, though their influence was by no means purely secular" (Israel Abrahams, art. "Jews," *Encyclopaedia Britannica,* 11th edition, Vol. 15, p. 403). The Patriarchate's emissaries (*Apostoli*) visited communities not only to collect taxes, but also to advise them on the conduct of their affairs, especially in matters of religion and education. About 226 C.E., the Church Father, Origen, wrote:

How much even now, where the Romans rule and the Jews pay to them the tribute, has the president of the

---

*Muir, l.c., pp. 233 ff. and 271 ff.

Mahomet appreciated perfectly the central place that Palestine occupied in the life of the Jewish people. So long as he hoped to win them over he recognized Jerusalem as the *Kibla,* "the Holy of Holies to which he and his people turned five times a day while they prostrated themselves in prayer" (Muir, p. 177). On realizing that this hope was vain, he—according to Mahommedan tradition—pleaded with the Lord that He "might change the direction of my face in prayer away from the Kibla of the Jews." A divine revelation pointed to Mecca as "a Kibla that shall please thee." (Muir, p. 183)

people among them in his power with permission of the Emperor? Even courts are secretly held according to the law, and even on various occasions sentence of death is pronounced. This I, who have long lived in the land of this people, have myself experienced and ascertained.

Mommsen, who quotes these words of Origen, adds:

Beyond question this patriarch was for the Jews the old *High Priest,* and thus the obstinate people of God had once more reconstituted themselves and in so far overthrown Vespasian's work.   (*Provinces,* Vol. II, p. 227)

And, we may add, Hadrian's also.

The Patriarchate remained in existence until the final dissolution by Theodosius II, in 425. By this act the last spark of recognized Jewish autonomy in Palestine was extinguished. "So long as they had a president and a Sanhedrin in the Holy Land they had a common country, though they had ceased to have a sacrifice, temples, a prophet or a king." (Rev. George Townsend, *The New Testament,* London, 1938, p. 483)

It was during this period that the two great collections of religious literature, the *Mishna* (end of 2nd century) and the *Talmud Yerushalmi* (end of 4th century), were compiled, hundreds of scholars and spiritual leaders contributing to the work. Cultural values of this kind are not created by a people entirely scattered and broken.

There was yet a third line of defense—revolt. The struggle against Hadrian was the last large-scale effort to throw off the Roman yoke attempted by the Jews, but it

was not by any means their last recourse to arms. Despite
the paucity of historical material, it is possible to discern
a definite line of political orientation guiding Jewish action
through the five centuries which elapsed between Bar-
Cochba and the Arab conquest of Palestine. On the whole,
the line followed that laid down in the Hasmonean period.
Jewish political thought was determined for centuries
by two basic ideas. The first was that Jewish independence
and Roman world power were incompatible. Caesarea
being then the center of Roman culture and administration in Palestine, a Jewish sage said in the third century:

Caesarea and Jerusalem—if one should tell thee that
both are destroyed, do not believe him; if he says both
are peopled, believe him not. If he say: Caesarea is
destroyed and Jerusalem is peopled, or Jerusalem is destroyed and Caesarea is peopled, believe him . . . When
the one is replenished, the other must be waste; both cannot flourish or be desolate at the same time.

The second idea guiding Jewish political thought was
that Parthia (Persia) was the only power that might be
expected to defeat Rome. "When you see the Powers
fighting each other," said Eleazar B'Rabbi Abina, "look
for the coming of the King Messiah." (*Bereshit Rabba,*
Ch. 42) The Powers to which he referred were Rome—
"the wicked power which levies troops from all nations
of the world" — and Parthia. The Talmud paid tribute
to Parthia's stand against Roman aggression by saying:
"Of the ten measures of courage that came down into the

world, the Persians received nine." (*Kiddushin* 49, col. 2)
"They [the Persians] are like the hosts of the House of
David" (*Kiddushin* 72, col. 1). "The destroyers of the
second Temple will fall into the hands of Persia," said
Rabbi Judah Ben-Ilai after the Bar-Cochba war. Rabbi
Jose Ben-Kisma instructed his family while on his death-
bed: "Bury me deep in the ground, for there will not be
a coffin in all Palestine that the Persians will not use as a
trough for their horses." And Rabbi Simon Ben-Jochai
said at the end of the second century: "When thou seest a
Persian steed tied to an Israelite tombstone, then canst
thou believe in the Messiah."

Jewish statesmanship had clearly conceived its own
problem as interwoven with the great struggle between
Orient and Occident.* It hoped for salvation from the
victory of the former.

———

*In Milton's *Paradise Regained,* Satan arguing with Jesus Christ
speaks of David's throne:—
> . . . how couldst thou hope
> Long to enjoy it, quiet and secure,
> Between two such enclosing enemies,
> Roman and Parthian? Therefore one of these
> Thou must make sure thy own; the Parthians first
> By my advice, as nearer, and of late
> Found able by invasion to annoy
> Thy country, and captive lead away her kings,
> Antigonus and old Hyrcanus, bound,
> Maugre the Roman: It shall be my task
> To render thee the Parthian at dispose,
> Choose which thou wilt, by conquest or by league:
> By him thou shalt regain, without him not,
> That which alone can truly re-install thee
> In David's royal seat, his true successor.
>   (*Paradise Regained,* Book III)

68

Apart from identity of interests, there was an important factor which contributed greatly to that Eastern orientation—the existence of a flourishing Jewish community in the Parthian empire. Accordingly, scarcely a quarter of a century after the defeat of Bar-Cochba, Antoninus Pius—who in 138 C.E. had annulled some of the most cruel of Hadrian's edicts—was compelled in 161 to send a military expedition to suppress a Jewish revolt in Palestine.

The attempt at a new call to arms appears to have been connected with the warlike preparations commenced by the Parthians against Rome. Though often deceived, the Judeans still hoped for the help of the Parthians (Persians) as a means of deliverance from the Roman yoke.

(H. Graetz, *History of the Jews,* Vol. II, p. 449)

In 175 C.E. the Emperor Marcus Aurelius encouraged his legions in the struggle against the rebel Cassius with the words: "The Cilicians, the Syrians, the Jews and the Egyptians have never proved your equals." He is also reported to have shown disapproval of the Jews by remarking: "At last I have discovered a people more restless than the Marcomani, the Quadi or the Sarmati" —peoples with whom he was then at war.

A quarter of a century later (201) the Emperor Septimius Severus had to wage regular war upon Jewish rebels in Palestine who had taken to arms in the hope of restoring Jewish independence while Rome was engaged in fighting Vologeses, King of Parthia. Victory over the Jews was adjudged by the Senate important enough to justify the granting to the Emperor of a "Jewish triumph."

In the middle of the fourth century (352), under the Byzantine Emperor Constantine, a Jewish rising once more broke out in Palestine, again timed to coincide with one of the chronic wars with Persia. In this the towns of Sephoris, Tiberias, Acre and Lydda took a prominent part; after the suppression of the revolt, they were destroyed.

In 362 Julian the Apostate, on the eve of his departure for the Persian war, promised the Jews to "reconstruct the holy city of Jerusalem" and the Temple at his own expense. This promise derived not only from the personal wish of the Emperor to discredit the Christian thesis that the destruction of the Temple proved the case for Christianity; it was a deliberate political move to win the sympathy and support of the Jews in Palestine and perhaps also in Persia. Church historians (Socrates and others) tell of the great joy with which this promise was greeted. In Jewish records, however, the episode is not even mentioned, probably because the Jews had no confidence in the permanency of this change in Roman policy and saw better prospects of restoration in a Persian victory.

The pro-Persian orientation appears to have been shared by the Jews of the diaspora. In the rivalry between the two empires, Yemen (then called *Khimyar*) played an important part. A foothold in that country would have meant to Byzantium vital strategic, as well as commercial, advantages in the area now commonly known as the Middle East, an alternative line of communication to

India when the road through Persia was closed, and a springboard for attack on Persia from the south. To achieve this purpose Byzantium used all possible methods of persuasion and compulsion, ranging from lavish gifts and promises of lucrative trade, to military invasions by Abyssinia, a vassal of the Byzantine empire. Even Christian proselytism was exploited as an agency for Byzantine foreign policy. The sympathies of the Jews of Yemen, whose reigning dynasty had embraced Judaism at the end of the fourth century, were with Persia, and the Christian-Jewish conflict in that part of the world was in a high degree a reflex of the Byzantine-Persian rivalry. The defeat of the Jewish ruler of Yemen, Dhu-Nuwas, and the conquest of the country by the Abyssinians in 525 was in fact a Byzantine victory over Persia. Fifty years later Yemen revolted and, with Persian help, expelled the invaders. But soon afterwards Persia herself occupied the country and held it until the Islamic conquest.

In the sixth century there were three revolts in Palestine against Byzantine rule—in 529, 556 and 578. Jews took an active part, together with Samaritans, in the two last. In 614 a Jewish army in Palestine was fighting Byzantium on the Persian side.

A war commenced between the Persian and Roman empires which proved the last and bloodiest of their numerous struggles; and its violence and strange vicissitudes contributed in a great degree to the dissolution of both these ancient monarchies.

71

The Roman armies, having lost their discipline, were everywhere defeated. Mesopotamia, Syria, Palestine, Phoenicia, Cappadocia, Galatea and Paphlagonia were laid waste . . . The emperor (Phocas) determined to prove his orthodoxy by ordering all the Jews in the empire to be baptized. The Jews, who formed a wealthy and powerful class in many of the cities of the East, resisted this act of oppression and caused a bloody sedition, which contributed much to aid the progress of the Persian armies.

. . . the deplorable condition of the Roman empire and of the Christian population in the East inspired the Jews with some expectations of soon re-establishing their national independence under the expected Messiah. It must be confessed that the desire of availing themselves of the misfortunes of the Roman empire, and of the dissensions of the Christian Church, was the natural consequence of the oppression to which they had been subjected . . .

(George Finley, *Greece under the Romans,*

pp. 305/6 and 320/21)

The Christian historian, Entychius (9th century), reports that "the Jews of Tiberias, the mountains of Galilee, Nazareth and the parts round about . . . went to Jerusalem and helped the Persians to destroy the Churches and murder the Christians" (*Eutychii Annales,* Palestine Pilgrims' Text Society Tracts, Vol. XI, p. 34).

When Heraclius reconquered the country in 628 he still thought it wise solemnly to promise the Jews safety. But having thus secured their sympathy, he broke his pledge at the instance of the Christian clergy and put many thousands of Jews to death. The Arab conquest, which followed a few years later (634-638)* was therefore welcomed and actively aided by the Jews.

UNDER ARAB RULE

Jews in Palestine made no more attempts to throw off the conqueror's yoke by force of arms. Their numbers had shrunk with every rising, for the revolts were always followed by mass murder, confiscation, deportation into slavery, expulsion, and flight into foreign lands. Nevertheless, even after the Arab conquest the Jewish population was not insignificant. The messianic hopes cherished in connection with that invasion very soon proved completely unjustified, though the treatment of the Jews was incomparably better under Arab rule than under Christian Byzantium. They enjoyed religious freedom, and for the first time in centuries the gates of Jerusalem were opened to them. They were even allowed to build a synagogue

---

*J. B. Bury (*History of the Later Roman Empire*) regards as one of the factors which determined the defeat of Heraclius "the continuation of an unfortunate policy which had already proved disastrous, the persecution of the Jews. They were massacred in Palestine, they were massacred also at Edessa, and were forced to flee to Arabia. We are tempted to think that but for this fatal error events might have taken a different course, for we can hardly overrate the importance of the Hebrews in those countries." (Book V, Vol. II, p. 246)

in the Temple area, by the Wailing Wall. But, on the other hand, the new rulers' land policy was calculated to displace them from the last remnant of their land.

The agricultural element was still strong in the Jewish population at the end of the Byzantine period. Numerous priestly families still made their living from *Trumoth*— offerings of field produce supplied to them by the peasants as in the days of the Temple, in anticipation of an early resumption of their functions. The Arab conquest brought into the country large numbers of land-hungry soldiers and desert tribes, who expected to be settled on the land. Omar I, immediately after the conquest, limited the new-comers to lands whence Byzantine owners had fled, or to which there were no heirs after the death of the owner. He even seems to have permitted Jews to reoccupy the areas confiscated from them by the Byzantines. But his successor Othman, and especially Mu'awijah, re-confis-cated a large portion of those lands for the settlement of Arabs, and this policy was pursued by later Khalifs.

In *Pirke de'Rabbi Eliezer,* fragment of a Midrashic work composed in the eighth century, this is hinted at in the form of a "prophecy" regarding what "the sons of Ishmael [the Arabs] will do in the land in the last days: they will measure the land with ropes, they will make the cemetery into a couching place of sheep on their dunghills, and they will measure them, and some of them [they will measure] on the tops of the mountains . . ." This can only mean that a very thorough land survey had been carried out both in the valleys and on the hills (where

the terracing system was still in existence), that not even
Jewish cemeteries were exempt, and that most, if not all,
of the land was given to the invading tribes and soldiers
and converted into pastures for their flocks. It was only
then that Jewish agriculture sank into insignificance and
the Jewish people definitely lost its grip on the land.

Although what remained of Jewish self-administration
was permanently lost in 425, "dejudaization" of the country was effected only two centuries later, after the Arab
conquest. The Byzantines under Theodosius completed
the process of political-administrative suppression of the
Jewish people begun by Pompey in 63 B.C.; the policy of
destroying the physical ties between Israel and its land
which Vespasian and Hadrian had initiated was brought
to its conclusion in the seventh century C.E. by the Arabs
under Mu'awijah and his successors.

A Jewish document dating from the second half of the
ninth century says:

It is an established rule with our Rabbis that there is
not one man in Israel who hath not four ells of ground in
the Land of Israel. And should it be asserted that the land
was seized by non-Jews several generations ago [then the
answer is that] it was established by our Rabbis that land
cannot be seized and the tenure of Israel continues valid.
(M. Assaf, *History of Arab Rule in Palestine*
[Hebrew], Tel-Aviv, 1935, p. 83)

The disturbances in the Moslem world, the Arab
invasion and the Crusades, the rivalries and struggles

between successive dynasties (Omayads, Abassids, Fatimids, Seljuks) contributed much to the impoverishment of Palestine, brought severe suffering to the Christians and greatly reduced the Jewish population. Yet, at the end of that period, urban Jewish communities in Jerusalem, Acre, Haifa, Jaffa, Ramle, Ascalon, Gaza and Akaba still survived. The Arab traveller, Mukadasi, complained at the end of the tenth century that in Jerusalem "everywhere the Christians and the Jews have the upper hand" (*Description of Syria, including Palestine,* Palestine Pilgrims Text Society, Vol. III, p. 87). And further: "In this province of Syria also for the most part the assayers of coin, the dyers, bankers and tanners are Jews, while it is most usual for the physicians and the scribes to be Christians" (p. 77).

Even Jewish agriculture was not yet entirely uprooted, especially in Galilee. It was about the middle of the eighth century, or even later, that Eleazar Kalir, a Palestinian poet, wrote the *Prayer for Dew,* which is part of Jewish liturgy to this day:

> Dew, precious dew, unto Thy land forlorn
> Pour out our blessings in Thy exultation,
> To strengthen us with ample wine and corn
> And give Thy chosen city safe foundation
>   In dew . . .*

---

*Israel Zangwill, *Voice of Jerusalem,* Heinemann, 1920.

Prayer for plenty of water and for a good crop — agricultural actuality speaks from these lines, actuality as living as that expressed in the prayer for deliverance from subjection and exile.

The three and a half centuries between the Arab invasion and the first Crusade constituted a period of fruitful spiritual and intellectual activity among Palestine Jews. In 640 the Academy of Tiberias was transferred to Jerusalem. In the seventh and eighth centuries the definitive edition of the text of the Scriptures was completed and the system of vowel points introduced. During that period the first *paytanim* (authors of *piyutim,* liturgical poems) appeared in Palestine, the most important being Eleazar Kalir. Although before that era Palestine had lost its hegemony in Jewish spiritual and religious life to the flourishing community of Babylon, at the end of the tenth century it aspired to regain its central position. But the attempt to transfer the authority of the Gaonate from Babylon to Palestine failed, the struggle between the great Babylonian *Gaon,* Saadyah, and the Palestinian, Rabbi Meir, ending in the former's favor. Nevertheless, that such a struggle had become possible, and that many of the European communities supported the claims of the Palestine Gaonate, is significant of the central importance which Palestine was beginning to regain in the eyes of the nation as a whole.

CHAPTER FIVE

Re-immigration

RE-IMMIGRATION OF JEWS INTO PALESTINE WENT ON un-interruptedly from the days of the Babylonian captivity. Talmudic and Arab sources show a considerable influx of Babylonian Jews in the second half of the second century and towards the end of the third. In 624-5, on the eve of the Arab invasion, the Jews of Beni-Canucaa and Beni-Nadhir (near Medina), defeated by Mahomet, migrated from Arabia to Adraat in Transjordan and Jericho. Omar I expelled all the Jews of the Hedjaz to Tema (in Northern Arabia*) and Jericho (640). Between the Arab conquest and the first Crusade, immigration of Jews from Babylon, Egypt, Syria (8th and 9th century), Africa, Spain (10th century), slowed down the decrease of the Jewish population.

But the first Crusade almost wiped out all the Jews

---

*This region was considered as belonging not to the Hedjaz but to "Ash-Sha'm," meaning the northern country, Syria and Palestine.

of Palestine. The Jews of Jerusalem were burned alive inside the synagogue, those of Haifa perished in defending the town. Large numbers had to flee the country. Yet already under the Latin Kingdom re-settlement began. Almost every century saw *Aliyoth* (waves of immigration), in numbers not large by present reckoning but very considerable if political and economic conditions and the difficulty and danger of travel in those times are taken into consideration.

In the course of generations, countless numbers of Jews went to Palestine at the close of their days, to be buried in the soil of their ancestral land. "What a testimony of the inextinguishable love of the country! In vain will it be denied," wrote Alphonse de Lamartine in 1832. And Karl Marx, in an article written on the outbreak of the Crimean War and published in the New York *Tribune* on April 15, 1854, said:

The sedentary population of Jerusalem numbers about 15,500 souls, of whom 4,000 are Mussulmans and 8,000 Jews. The Mussulmans, forming about a fourth part of the whole and consisting of Turks, Arabs, and Moors, are, of course, the masters in every respect, as they are in no way affected by the weakness of their Government at Constantinople. Nothing equals the misery and the sufferings of the Jews at Jerusalem, inhabiting the most filthy quarter of the town, called Hareth-el-Yahoud, in the quarter of dirt between the Zion and the Moriah, where their synagogues are situated—the constant objects of Mussulman oppression and intolerance, insulted by the

Greeks, persecuted by the Latins, and living only upon the scanty alms transmitted by their European brethren. The Jews, however, are not natives, but from different and distant countries, and are only attracted to Jerusalem by the desire of inhabiting the Valley of Jehosophat and dying on the very place where the redemption is to be expected.

(From a collection of Marx's articles,
The Eastern Question, London, 1897)

Some of the most illustrious men in Jewish history, religious leaders, scholars, philosophers, poets, cabbalistic dreamers, statesmen, were among those who found peace of mind and purpose in life by settling in the land of Israel. These included Yehuda Halevi, philosopher and poet, author of the immortal *Zionides* (twelfth century); Moses Ben Nahman (Nahmanides), Bible commentator and philosopher, rebuilder of the Jerusalem community (thirteenth century); Obadia of Bertinoro, the Mishna commentator (fifteenth century); Joseph Caro, author of the great law compendium *Shulkhan Arukh* (sixteenth century); Isaiah Halevi Hurwitz, cabbalistic authority (seventeenth century); Moshe Hayim Luzzatto, poet and cabbalistic authority (eighteenth century); the cabbalists, Shalom Sharaby (Yemen) and Hayim Ben-Athar (Morocco) in the same century.

The immigration of individuals, families, and small groups, went on practically without interruption year after year. There is also evidence of larger group immigrations, though obviously the records of only some of

80

these have survived. Here are typical instances. In 1211 three hundred Jews came from France and England; in 1495 several hundred, mainly from Sicily. At the end of the fourteenth century and during the sixteenth, some thousands entered from Spain, Portugal, Italy, etc., largely as a result of expulsions from the Iberian Peninsula. Naples (1539) and the Papal State (1569). In 1700, about 1,500 Jews from Poland, Hungary and Moravia left for Palestine, but only some 1,000 arrived, the others having perished on the way. In 1777, three hundred Hassidim with their families came to Palestine from Poland. 1812 saw the immigration of over four hundred followers of the *Wilna Gaon* from Lithuania. Some four hundred Jews from Galicia and Bucovina set out for Palestine in 1869. 1882 marked the beginning of the new era, leading up to the planned immigration of our own days.

The most important of these migrations before the inception of Zionism, was that of the sixteenth century, thanks to which Jerusalem, Hebron, Tiberias, and especially Safed became strong communities contributing many leaders to the spiritual life of the nation. This growth of the Jewish population inspired attempts to reestablish Palestine as the center of the Jewish world. Thus, Rabbi Jacob Berab — an immigrant from Spain — urged the setting-up of the Sanhedrin as the highest religious world authority. Don Joseph Naxos, a Jewish statesman, tried to establish in Tiberias and its vicinity a semi-autonomous Jewish agricultural and industrial settlement—an attempt sanctioned by the Sultan.

The Sanhedrin idea met with strong internal opposition, but the Tiberias settlement plan seemed at first to have good chances of success. The rebuilding of the town was begun, and calls went out to Jews, especially farmers and artisans, to come and settle in Tiberias. Ships were sent to Venice and Ancona to fetch the settlers. At least one community (Cori) is known to have prepared its collective transfer. But the whole plan had soon to be given up, mainly because the Turkish Government withdrew its consent.

The urge to go to Palestine could not always be satisfied. Frequently the plans of travellers were frustrated by shipwreck, pirates and the hostility of the same Christian forces that made life unbearable for Jews in Europe. Moreover, rulers were unwilling to lose the important source of income represented by the taxes, fines and other exactions, including wholesale confiscations) so often levied upon their Jewish subjects.

In 1286 a large group of Jews from Mainz, Worms, Speir and Oppenheim attempted secretly to emigrate to Palestine via Italy. They were caught, and, by order of the Emperor Rudolf, their leader, Rabbi Meir of Rothenburg, was thrown into prison, there to spend the rest of his life. The others had their houses and other immovable property impounded for the Imperial treasury. In 1392 a boat owned by Christians on its way from Barcelona to Alexandria and Beyruth was intercepted by order of the Spanish authorities, because it carried Marranos to Palestine.* In 1428 Pope Martin V, at the instigation of the Franciscan monks in Jerusalem, issued a Bull forbidding Christian skippers to carry Jewish passengers to Palestine. The Doge of Venice followed suit with a similar order to all ships sailing from Venetian ports. Ten years later it was decreed that any Jew found on board ship was to be thrown into the sea, and this order remained in force for fifty years. It was copied by the King of Naples. It is only fair, however, to mention that Popes Paul III, in 1543, and Gregory XIII, in 1581, ordered the population of Italy to treat kindly and to extend help to Jews leaving Italy for Palestine.

In 1455 Sicily witnessed a strong movement for emigration to Palestine. Groups of prospective emigrants were organized in Palermo, Messina, Catania, Syracuse, Termini, Minca, Ragusa. The Government got wind of it and declared all who were planning to leave guilty of violating the law banning the export of gold and other precious metals. They were condemned to death, and all their property confiscated; the sentence being subsequently commuted to a fine of one thousand ounces of gold.†

Polish sources report a Jewish emigration movement to Palestine in the thirties of the sixteenth century, evidently resulting from the messianic upheaval around Shlomo

---

*J. Baer, *History of the Jews in Christian Spain* [Hebrew], Tel-Aviv, 1945, p. 402.) See M. A. Shulvas, *Rome and Jerusalem* (Hebrew), Jerusalem, 1944.
†See M. A. Shulvas, *Rome and Jerusalem* (Hebrew), Jerusalem, 1944.

Molkho. This emigration seems to have been so widespread that the Jews were accused of exporting their fortunes to Turkey. King Sigismond I ordered a special investigation to be made, in the course of which many leaders of Jewish communities were arrested under suspicion of treason to the state and had to pay enormous sums to buy their release.*

In 1777 a law was drafted in Poland forbidding Jews to cross the Turkish frontier without a travelling document issued by Jewish community authorities. The frontier guards were to be instructed to prevent such illegal crossings of the frontier "on the way to Jerusalem." At the same time the Jewish communities were to be warned that they would have to pay taxes according to quotas previously fixed and that the decrease in their population owing to this illegal emigration would not be taken into account. It is not known whether this draft ever became law.

As late as 1812 the Austrian Government instructed the Governor of Galicia to prevent the pilgrimage and emigration of Jews to Palestine. Shortly afterwards Emperor Francis I directed the Austrian consuls in Constantinople and Odessa to refuse passports for Palestine to Austrian Jews. The rabbis and leaders of communities were to be held responsible if this emigration did not cease.

---

*See Dr. Ignacy Schipper, *The Polish-Lithuanian Jews and Palestine,* (in Polish), Vienna, 1917, p. 11.
†N. M. Gelber, *Plans for a Jewish State* (Hebrew), Knesseth, Tel-Aviv, 1939, p. 291

Cease it did not, and in 1883 the Turkish Government introduced the "Red Certificate" which was issued to every new arrival and required him to leave the country within three months. This rule remained in force until the first World War. Thus the entire Jewish immigration from the early eighties of the last century to the first World War estimated at between 50,000 and 70,000 souls, was "illegal."

It was as a result of this continuous Jewish homecoming that the Jewish population never disappeared entirely from the land of Israel, despite wars, epidemics, natural calamities, invasions by nomads from the desert. Despite repeated catastrophes and difficulties, the Jewish population constantly replenished itself.

BONDS BETWEEN THE DIASPORA AND PALESTINE

The attachment of the Jews of all countries to Palestine was shown by the continuous flow of financial aid to the Jewish community there. The contribution of Diaspora Jewry for the upkeep of the Temple, and later for the Patriarchate and Sanhedrin, have already been mentioned. The abolition of the Patriarchate in the fifth century did not stop this flow. Wherever there was a Jewish population of any size, regular collections were made for the support of religious and social institutions in Palestine and for the poor of the Holy Land. "Messengers of Zion" visited the lands of the dispersion at regular intervals to collect the money, to maintain contact between the Palestinian community and the Diaspora, and to give authentic information and guidance on matters Palestinian. In some countries — Italy, Germany, France, and elsewhere — special officials were regularly appointed to organize and administer the collections. The titles by which they were known (*President for Eretz-Israel* and *Treasurer for Eretz-Israel*) indicated the degree of importance attached to their office.

In Poland during the sixteenth century the officially recognized representative body of the Jewish population ("Synod of the Four Countries") introduced an official tax, "Coin for the Holy Land," for the collection of which the local communities were responsible. The amounts thus collected were used both for the support of Palestine pilgrims and for the maintenance of schools and the relief of the poor in Palestine. In this case the accusation was again raised against the Jews that they were helping Turkey to the detriment of the Polish State.* When, after the dissolution of Jewish communal autonomy (1764), taxation for Palestine came to an end, a new system of voluntary collections ("Halukah") was organized, which soon spread into other countries and for many decades played an important role in the economic life of the Jewish community in Palestine.†

*Schipper, l.c., p. 14.

Collection boxes were placed in synagogues and private houses — *"Eretz Israel* boxes" or "Boxes of Rabbi Meir Baal-Haness" — and every family used to make a weekly offering. Early in the nineteenth century, Sir Moses Montefiore was the pioneer protagonist of the idea that the offerings of Diaspora Jewry be used to make the Palestine community self-supporting through encouragement of manual labor, especially agriculture. This approach was later to be the central idea behind the extensive colonization supported by Baron Edmond de Rothschild and the "Lovers of Zion" groups in several countries. Their activities in the last two decades of the nineteenth century and the early years of the twentieth laid the foundations for the constructive work of modern Zionism.

LONGING FOR ZION

Self-taxation for Palestine was merely one concrete proof of the devotion which the Jewish people never ceased to feel for its historic homeland. The intensity of this devotion has varied in different countries and changing historical circumstances, but never, anywhere, did it dis-

---

†In the seventeenth century the Jewish community of Venice introduced an obligatory Palestine tax amounting to a quarter-ducat in gold in addition to the yearly communal tax of three or more ducats.

appear entirely. It colored the whole of Jewish life. In the daily prayers, in customs and religious observances, longing for the land and hope of return were dominant themes. Throughout the centuries, Israel day after day proclaimed before God and man his faithfulness to Zion. The longing for Zion inspired some of the loftiest creations of Jewish poetry.

> Zion, wilt thou not ask if peace's wing
>> Shadows the captives that ensue thy peace,
> Left lonely from thine ancient shepherding?
>
> Lo! west and east and north and south—world-wide—
>> All those from far and near, without surcease,
> Salute thee: Peace and Peace from every side;
>
> And Peace from him that from the captive's fount
>> Of tears, is giving his like Hermon's dew,
> And longing but to shed them on thy mount.
>
> I with the jackal's wail have mourned thee long,
>> But dreaming of thine own restored anew
> I am a harp to sound for thee thy song.*

These lines are recited every year on the ninth day of the month of Ab (Tisha be'Ab); the day on which there took place, according to tradition, the destruction of both the First and the Second Temple as well as the fall of the fortress of Bethar at the end of the Bar-Cochba revolt. This day is observed by Jews all over the world as a day of national mourning.

---

*From Yehuda Halevi's *Ode to Zion, Selected Poems,* translated by Nina Salaman, Jewish Publication Society, Philadelphia

Re-immigration

On the lordly heights of Zion,
Where the golden fortress towered
To the heavens, bearing witness
To a mighty monarch's power.

There, where only weeds are growing,
Everything's in ashy ruins,
So cast down and so pathetic
That, one thinks, the stones must weep.

And they do weep on occasion,
Once in every year, on every
Ninth of Ab the stones are mourning . . .
(Heinrich Heine, Yehuda Halevi)

"I cannot" — wrote Moses Hess, the forerunner of Socialist Zionism, in *Rome and Jerusalem* (1862) — "remember ever being more deeply moved than by the scenes which I witnessed in my grandfather's house in Bonn on the approach of the day of the destruction of Jerusalem. In the first nine days of the month of Ab the mourning which had commenced three weeks before this disastrous Ninth of Ab assumed a gloomy character. Even the Sabbath lost its festiveness during these days of national mourning, and it is characteristically designated the 'Black Sabbath.' "

"The most beautiful, the most glorious day in the life of a people is the day on which the whole people fasts," exclaimed Adam Mickiewicz, the great Polish poet, after he had witnessed the service on the Ninth of Ab (11th

August), 1845, in the synagogue in the Rue Notre Dame de Nazareth in Paris. In the invitation to members of his group to visit the synagogue on that occasion he wrote:

. . . We are bound up with the mourning of Israel who in every corner of the globe weep today for the desolation of Jerusalem. We Poles must rouse similar feelings in ourselves when we remember the massacre in Praga [in 1831, when Cossacks massacred thousands of people in that suburb of Warsaw] and the capture of Warsaw. To the French it is Waterloo. Come, let us bow down before the people of Israel which has for eighteen centuries known how to keep alive its anguish as if the disaster occurred only yesterday.

Throughout the centuries, in times of relative quiet and prosperity no less than in times of distress, the Diaspora was regarded merely as an interlude between the national past and a national future in the Land of Israel. For centuries the Jewish people was in a mental state comparable to that of a man compelled by circumstances temporarily to abandon his home: such a man is still mentally at home, though living outside of it. In the words of Yehuda Halevi: "My heart is in the East, and I am at the end of the West."

CHAPTER SIX

Messianism

Three watches has the night
And at each watch the Holy One,
Blessed be He, stands and roars
Like a lion:
Ah, woe is Me,
I have destroyed My house,
I have burned My temple,
And I have scattered My children
Among the nations of the world.

(Midrash)

"ON THE DAY when the Temple was destroyed the Messiah was born," says the Talmud. The messianic belief was elevated into one of the main tenets of the Jewish faith: "I believe with perfect faith in the coming of the Messiah, and though he tarry I will wait daily for his coming."

In secular terms, this messianic hope meant that the Jewish people never accepted permanent separation from its country. A typical statement of this attitude was made in a letter which Hasdai Ibn Shaprut, adviser to the Khalif Abdar-Rahman III of Andalusia in the tenth century, wrote to Joseph, ruler of the Jewish kingdom of the Khazars. "We indeed, who are the remnants of the captive Israelites . . . are dwelling peacefully in the land of our sojourning," Ibn-Shaprut asserts. He describes his own high position at court, and then turns with enthusiasm to the joyful tidings which had just reached him of a Khazar country where the Jews "form one independent kingdom and are not subject to any foreign ruler." He goes on: "If I could learn that this was the case, then, despising all my glory, abandoning my high estate, leaving my family, I would go over mountains and hills, through seas and lands, till I should arrive at the place where my Lord King resides, that I might see not only his glory and magnificence, and that of his servants and ministers, but also the tranquillity of the Israelites . . ."

But this is by no means all that he desires. He asks the King "whether there is among you any computation concerning the final redemption which we have been awaiting so many years, whilst we went from one captivity to another, from one exile to another. How strong is the hope of him who awaits the realization of these events. And, oh, how can I hold my peace and be at rest in the face of the desolation of the home of our glory . . . ?"

This longing for national restoration always—ever since

Isaiah and Micah—went hand in hand with hope for the moral regeneration of mankind, for peace between nations and for social justice. We find these aspects of messianism in the Book of Daniel, written during the Maccabean war in the second century B.C.; in the apocalyptic writings; in Talmud and Midrash; in Kabbalah and Hassidism, leading up to modern Zionism.

This is how Maimonides defined the messianic ideal in the twelfth century:

The Sages and Prophets did not long for the days of the Messiah in order to dominate the entire world, or rule over the heathens, or be exalted by the peoples, or to eat and drink and rejoice. Their desire was to be free to devote themselves to the Torah and its wisdom, without anyone to oppress and disturb them, in order that they might merit the life of the world to come. In that era there will not be famine or war, jealousy or strife.

Jewish mysticism dreamed of the salvation of the whole world in the Kingdom of God. The Jewish New Year service contains prayers for the time when all men "will form one league." "The saints will see and will rejoice, and the just will be glad, and the righteous will sing songs of praise, and injustice will shut its mouth, and all evil will end like smoke, because Thou wilt destroy the rule of evil in the world."

The more desperate the situation of the people, the remoter the chance of immediate deliverance, the more fanciful the messianic expectations projected into the future. Right through the ages, beginning with the first apocalyptic writings, the people's impatience vented itself in speculations as to the exact time when the coming of the Messiah might be expected. On the basis of certain passages in Scripture, especially the Book of Daniel, by combining the number values of certain letters in the Hebrew alphabet, and by other methods, Jews tried to lift the veil of the future and even to force the hand of Providence. In view of the constant disappointment they met, their spiritual leaders tried to discourage and even to forbid those speculations, but without lasting success.

Even more significantly, messianism did not always remain a matter of contemplation and longing. A whole chain of movements was created by so-called false Messiahs who during periods of severe persecution or world political upheavals, appeared time and again, kindling hopes of immediate redemption.

In some of these pseudo-Messiahs the tradition of armed struggle still lived. Abu Isa of Ispahan in the seventh century, Serene of Syria in the eighth, and David Alroy as late as the twelfth, all expected heavenly intervention but made plans for the military reconquest of Palestine. David Reubeni and his disciple and successor Shlomo Molkho, in the sixteenth century, tried to win the Christian world to a military alliance with an alleged Jewish kingdom in the East with the object of dislodging the Moslem rulers from the Holy Land. The others, conscious of the physical and political helplessness of their people, based all their hopes and promises on mystical speculations and miraculous formulae, without definite plans of action.

Not a century went by without one or more pseudo-Messiahs appearing, now in Crete, now in France, Spain, Morocco, Germany, Italy, Poland, Turkey, Palestine. The most important was Sabbatai Zevi in the middle of the seventeenth century. His appearance, against the background of the millenarian commotions in Europe arising out of the Thirty Years War, and of the sanguinary Chmielnicki pogroms in Eastern Europe, stirred a wave of messianic fervor throughout Jewry and even in non-Jewish circles. In Egypt, Syria, Turkey, Poland, Germany, Holland and England, Jews in all earnestness commenced preparations for departure to Palestine. Pepys records in his *Diary* that bets of 10 to 1 were being laid on the recognition of Sabbatai Zevi as Messiah in the year 1666. Henry Oldenburgh, Secretary of the Royal Society, wrote to Spinoza on December 8, 1665: "Here there is a rumor in everybody's mouth that the Jews . . . are to return to their country." And, though sceptical himself, he asks Spinoza to tell him what he hears and thinks about this matter.*

The Jewess, Glueckel of Hamelin, in her famous *Memoirs*, describes the joy with which the tidings concerning

---

*Spinoza's reply is not on record. But in his *Tractatus Theologico-Politicus* (published 1670) he says: "I would go so far as to believe that, if the foundations of their religion have not enfeebled their minds, they may, if the occasion presents itself amid the changes to which human affairs are so liable, even raise up their empire anew, and that God may elect them a second time."

Sabbatai Zevi were received by the Jews — especially the Sephardic community — of Hamburg. She sadly concludes: "Some of them unfortunately sold all they had — home, land and possessions, hoping to be redeemed any day."

The *Calendar of State Papers for 1665-6** reports on February 5, 1666, a petition of a Jew of Amsterdam to the King "for a pass for a Holland ship to transport himself and fifty families of Jews from Amsterdam to Palestine." The same source reports, under the date of March 15, 1666: "The Jews hurry from Amsterdam with great expectation of their Messias."

Nor was this the first phenomenon of its kind.

There was an extensive Messianic movement in Germany, Byzantium and the country of the Khazars in the year 1096.† That year had been considered by some "calculators of the end" as the year of the prospective advent of the Messiah. As it happened, it coincided with the beginning of the first Crusade, which brought unprecedented suffering to the Jewish people wherever the Crusaders set foot. These sufferings, in turn, were considered by many as the "pangs of the Messiah." According to a report found in the *Genizah* (depository of defunct sacred books and documents) at Cairo, in 1096, German Jews

---

*Ed. Mary Anne Everett Green, Domestic Series, London, 1864; quoted by Abba Hillel Silver, *Messianic Speculation in Israel*, New York, 1927, pp. 182-3.
†See: David Kaufmann, *A Hitherto Unknown Messianic Movement*, Jewish Quarterly Review, 1897-8, pp. 139 ff; Abba Hillel Silver, l.c., pp. 77-8.

started off for Palestine by way of Byzantium "in masses numbering many thousands with their wives and children and all their possessions." In Khazaria seventeen communities are said to have left their homes and marched into the desert in the hope of there meeting the lost ten tribes and, together with them, marching on to the Holy Land. The Jews of France despatched a special messenger to Constantinople to obtain information on whether the time of deliverance had actually arrived.

Even the Christians in the Byzantine Empire appear to have been affected by the wave of Messianic excitement. The Emperor and the Patriarch encouraged the Jews to sell their houses and chattels and follow the Messianic call.

A similar movement a bare century and a half later is reported by the sixteenth century Czech historian, Hayek. In 1235, evidently under the impact of the movement of Mongolian hordes from Asia to the West, the Jews of Prague received letters from "countries of the South" saying that the Messiah had been born thirty years before and that "Gog and Magog," who had been confined by Alexander the Great in the mountains of the Caspian Sea, had started off to meet the Jews of the North. The Jews reacted by liquidating their immovable goods and buying weapons. One day they left the Ghetto and assembled outside the city in expectation of the enemy. King Wenceslas I intervened and stopped the movement.*

*See: Dr. Ignacy Schipper, *The Polish-Lithuanian Jews and Palestine* (in Polish), Vienna, 1917, and *A Messianic Movement in Prague,* in the Hebrew monthly *Gilyonot,* Tel-Aviv, 1939, p. 410.

"Liberal" historians often label these pseudo-Messiahs as impostors. Impostors some may have been: but others genuinely believed themselves chosen to lead the Jewish people back to the land of their fathers. Perhaps in the majority of cases both elements were present — light and darkness intermingled.† Essentially, whether they were impostors or not, the real question is not why they thought it their mission to lead the Jews back to Palestine, but why the Jews accepted the idea. Why did such great movements spring up among the Jews? "Like one who wanders in the dark of night," says a Midrash, "now and then kindling a light to brighten his path, only to have it again and again extinguished by the wind, until at last he resolves to wait patiently for the break of day when he will no longer require a light, so were the people of Israel with their would-be deliverers who appeared from time to time, only to delude their hopes; until they exclaimed at last, 'In Thy light alone, oh Lord, do we see light.' "

---

†The "Besht," founder of the Hassidic movement, said of Sabbatai Zevi that there had been in him "a holy spark, but Satan had caught him in his net." (*The Hassidic Anthology*, ed. Louis Newman, New York, 1934, Introduction, p. LXXII)

CHAPTER SEVEN

The Attitude of the Gentile World

THAT THE JEWS MAINTAINED AN UNBROKEN connection with Palestine is indisputable. History and literature are emphatic on a parallel point as well. They tell us that in the minds of the Gentiles, friends and enemies alike, the Jewish connection with Palestine remained a living fact throughout the centuries of Jewish dispersion.

This is confirmed by the Christian conception that the expulsion of the Jews from Palestine was a divine punishment for their refusal to accept Christianity and for their treatment of its founder. Christendom thus tried to find an explanation for the extraordinary phenomenon of the homeless "wandering Jew", as well as an excuse for its own behavior towards him.

"It was not by their own power that the Caesars did what they did to you; it was done by the wrath of God and His absolute rejection of you." Thus Chrysostom in the fourth century, who then goes on to argue that God would never allow the Jews to rebuild their Temple or to return to Jerusalem.

The theme is repeated through the ages, and in the seventeenth century we find Pascal writing:

It is a wonderful thing, and worthy of all attention, to see the Jewish nation existing so many years in constant misery, it being necessary as a proof of Jesus Christ, both that they should exist to be His witness, and should be miserable because they crucified Him, and though to be miserable and to exist, are contradictory, this nation still exists in spite of its misery . . . the second destruction is without promise of restoration . . . they are captives without hope.

Christendom admitted, as a corollary, that this separation from its homeland was, for the homeless people, a disaster—one that it had deserved, yet nevertheless a terrible disaster for a people that had lost its home, and had not forgotten and never would forget it. For were it otherwise—could it forget—then the punishment would not be a punishment at all.

But the Christian world did not always and everywhere uphold this doctrine of finality. Particularly after the beginning of the seventeenth century, voices began to be heard which refused to reconcile themselves to the idea that the Jewish tragedy would never end, and foretold the reunion of the people and the land in the near or distant future. Some, like Milton in his *Paradise Regained,* linked

100

the return with the conversion of the Jews to Christianity. Others held that the return of the Jewish people to Palestine must precede the millennium; and the sympathy shown by many people in England for Manasseh Ben-Israel's efforts to bring about the readmission of the Jews to that country derived from their belief that the Jews must first be dispersed in *all* countries before they could return to their own land.

The opinion of many Christians and mine doe concurre herein, that we both believe that the restoring time of our Nation into their Native Countrey is very near at hand; I believing more particularly, that this restauration cannot be, before these words of Daniel, Chap. 12, ver. 7, be first accomplished, when he saith, "And when the dispersion of the Holy people shall be compleated in all places, then shall all these things be compleated": signifying therewith, that before all be fulfilled, the People of God must be first dispersed into all places and Countreyes of the World. Now we know, how our Nation at the present is spread all about, and hath its seat and dwelling in the most flourishing parts of all the Kingdomes, and the Countreys of the World, as well in America, as in the other three parts thereof; except onely in this considerable and mighty Island. And therefore this remains onely in my judgement, before the Messia come and restore our Nation, that first we must have our seat here likewise. (From *A Declaration to the Commonwealth of England, by Rabbi Menasseh Ben Israel, Shewing the Motives of his Coming into England,* reprinted in *Menasseh Ben Israel's Mission to Oliver Cromwell,* edited by Lucien Wolf—Jewish Historical Society publication, 1901, p. 79)

It was certainly no accident that this idea became so prevalent at the end of the sixteenth and the beginning of the seventeenth centuries. It was closely connected with the upheavals that occurred in Europe at that time, and more especially with the grave situation in which the Jews found themselves in a number of countries. The appearance of the "false Messiahs", David Reubeni and Shlomo Molkho in the sixteenth century, and of Sabbatai Zevi in the seventeenth, not only convulsed Jewish life but also aroused intense interest in the outside world. The disturbances of the Thirty Years War, which to many seemed a sign of the coming of the End of Days, and the persecutions of the Jews (from the expulsion from Spain in the West to the Chmelnicki massacres in the East of Europe), compelled the best minds in Christendom to give serious consideration to the position of the Jewish people. During the two and a half centuries that elapsed between the Sabbatai Zevi movement and modern Zionism there was a long line of non-Jewish theologians, poets, thinkers and statesmen who realised the tragedy of Jewish homelessness and tried, each in his own way, to devise means of reuniting the Jews with the mother soil of Palestine.

Each century in its own way. In the seventeenth century Christian conversionist speculations centered on the expectation of Jewish redemption linked with the idea of the Jews correcting their historic error in respect of Christianity. A representative publication of this period is characteristically entitled *The World's Great Restoration, or The Calling of the Jews and with Them of All the Nations and Kingdoms of the Earth to the Faith of Christ* (Sir Henry Finch, London, 1621); it foretells that "the Jews and all Israel shall return to their land and ancient seats, conquer their foes, have their soil more fruitful than ever. They shall erect a glorious Church in the Land of Judah itself and bear rule far and near." During this period there is no call for action of any kind, but only speculations concerning the fulfillment of the Biblical prophecies by Divine power.

The eighteenth century continued this trend of Christian speculative thought*, but there were already attempts to suggest a program of activities which would make it possible to realize the plans of redemption. In 1695 a Danish merchant, Holger Pauli, submitted to the Kings of England and France and other monarchs a plan for the restoration of the Jewish State in Palestine. Several similar projects were put forward during the eighteenth century, as well as a number of "territorialist" proposals. In 1799 Napoleon Bonaparte issued a proclamation to the "rightful heirs of Palestine" inviting them to "take over what has been conquered and . . . to maintain it against all comers." And presently the idea of giving back Palestine to the Jewish people became a serious consideration

---

* Rousseau was ahead of his time. "I do not think," he wrote in 1762, "I have ever heard the arguments of the Jews as to why they should not have a free state, schools and universities, where they can speak and argue without danger. Then alone can we know what they have to say." (*Emile,* Everyman Edition, p. 268)

in international politics. About 1840 the statesmen of the Great Powers, at the initiative of Lord Shaftesbury and of the British Prime Minister, Lord Palmerston, seriously discussed such a proposal both as a means of grappling with the Jewish question and as an attempt to deal with the problem of the political future of Palestine, which was then in the melting pot. In the course of the nineteenth century Russian Decabrists, Polish Liberationists (Lelewel, Mickiewicz), and French and British statesmen came to think of the restoration of Jewish Palestine not only as the answer to the Jewish question, but—some of them, at least—also as the logical outcome of the liberation of Greece and Italy. It is not chance that the same Lord Byron who fought and was killed fighting for Greek liberation, wrote the lines:

> The wild-dove hath her nest, the fox his cave,
> Mankind their country—Israel but the grave!

From Byron a direct line leads to Disraeli and George Eliot.

The vineyards of Israel have ceased to exist, but the eternal law enjoins the children of Israel still to celebrate the vintage. A race that persist in celebrating their vintage, although they have no fruits to gather, will regain their vineyards. (Disraeli, *Tancred*)

Revive the organic centre; let the unity of Israel which has made the growth and form of its religion be an outward reality. Looking towards a land and a polity, our dispersed people in all the ends of the earth may share the dignity of a national life which has a voice among the people of the East and the West—which will plant the wisdom and skill of our race so that it may be, as of old, a medium of transmission and understanding. . . . And the world will gain as Israel gains. (George Eliot, *Daniel Deronda*)

Laurence Oliphant did not stop at literary expressions of sympathy, but devoted the last decade of his life—joined by his wife Alice—to practical efforts to facilitate Jewry's return to Zion. With the sympathetic knowledge of the British Government, he negotiated with Turkey, and then settled in Palestine, helping in the first stages of modern Jewish colonization (1880-1888).*

---

*An extensive review of Christian (especially English) Zionism is contained in N. Sokolow's *History of Zionism* (2 Vol.), London, 1919. See also Dr. Franz Kobler's article: *The Historical Antecedents* in *The Jewish National Home,* edited by Paul Goodman, London, 1943, and Albert M. Hyamson, *British Projects for the Restoration of the Jews,* published by the British Palestine Committee, London, 1917.

CHAPTER EIGHT

Historical Connection and Historical Right

WE HAVE SEEN THAT THE JEWISH PEOPLE HAS, over a period of centuries, not only preserved its historical connection with Palestine, but also continued to believe in its historic right to return there. We have seen, too, that in the course of centuries many of the finest and most far-seeing minds among non-Jews have come to the conclusion that the ultimate answer to the Jewish problem is the satisfaction of this right to return. When the preamble to the Palestine Mandate says that "recognition has thereby been given to the historical connection of the Jewish people with Palestine and to the grounds for reconstituting their national home in that country," it voices not a new conception but the logical conclusion of a long chain of history.

Yet the question must be faced whether this subjective

historical connection is a legitimate ground for establishing the *historical right* of the Jewish people to Palestine. Is not this right revoked by the right of the Arab people, which has been living in the country for centuries?

We often hear the argument: there was a period in history when Britain was under Roman rule; does that give the Italians the right to claim England for themselves? Can the Arabs, who were once dominant in Spain, now claim Spain as their land? The answer is, of course, a categorical negative. But these cases cannot be compared with that of the Jews. Suppose that Spain had played the same role in the life of the Arabs as a nation throughout their history that Palestine has played in the life of the Jewish people; suppose that the Arabs were in the same need of a country as the Jewish people is; suppose further that they could show that their entry into Spain would not be detrimental to the existing population; that the Spanish nation has vast undeveloped and under-populated territories at its disposal. Then the Arab claim to Spain would be irresistible indeed.

"Historical right" is a somewhat discredited conception in the democratic, and, above all, in the Socialist world. Too often in the course of history it has been made to serve as a blind for wars of conquest and territorial annexations, and as a pretext for retaining conquered territories against the wishes of the population. "Historical right" has thus become the antithesis of the democratic principle of national self-determination. And it is only natural that many progressive people should have had, and still have, difficulty in reconciling their negation of "historical rights" with support of Zionism.

But here again the unique nature of the Jewish case must be considered. The term "historical right" is discredited, obviously not because of its historical character but because the conception has so often in history been misused in an attempt to justify injustice. It is utterly wrong to suppose that every claim to historical right must *per se* be spurious. We must always first examine the actual substance of the supposed right and discover what it really means.

The Jewish aim is not to establish an alien rule over the population and the resources of the country for the benefit of an outside Power, but to replant in its ancient home the people that was uprooted from it; not to dominate and to exploit it from without, but to come there to live and to work on the land, to build and develop it, to restore it and in doing so to be itself restored; not to conquer a colony for a foreign "motherland," but to build up a home and a fatherland for a homeless people. Is it not obvious that a deep gulf lies between the two conceptions?

A historical claim, capable, if granted, of solving the problem of a great historic people, can be questioned only if it conflicts with rights and interests of greater magnitude and validity; if, in other words, it cannot be realized without committing a grave injustice against another people. Only if it could be shown that Jewish immigration and colonization did harm to the Arab people would there

108

be any ground for questioning whether the Jewish historical right is sufficiently strong to validate the Jewish claim.

Is this the case?

Before the first World War, Palestine was a country of Arab emigration. Since then the Arab population has grown from 600,000 to over one million—an increase which not one of the neighboring Arab countries has been able to equal. This fact alone should dispose of the myth of "displacement of Arabs" by Jewish immigration. The Palestine Royal Commission declared:

Up till now the Arab cultivator has benefited on the whole both from the work of British administration and from the presence of Jews in the country. Wages have gone up; the standard of living has improved; work on roads and buildings has been plentiful. In the Maritime plain some Arabs have adopted improved methods of cultivation.

(Report of Palestine Royal Commission, 1937, p. 241)

The general beneficent effect of Jewish immigration on Arab welfare is illustrated by the fact that the increase in Arab population is most marked in urban areas affected by Jewish development. A comparison of the census returns in 1922 and 1931 shows that, six years ago, the increase per cent in Haifa was 86, in Jaffa 62, in Jerusalem 37, while in purely Arab towns such as Nablus and Hebron it was only 7, and at Gaza there was a decrease of 2 per cent.

(l.c., p. 129)

True, the Jewish population has grown much more quickly (from less than one tenth to one third of the population), and its continuing growth on a scale commensurate with the unprecedented need of the Jewish people must result in a Jewish majority in the near future. Is this not unjust to the Arab nation? Have the Arabs not the right to say: "It is true that you do not harm us; on the contrary, economically we derive benefits from your immigration and reconstruction work. But we don't want your benefits, which are bound to result in our being converted into a minority. We are not prepared to pay for economic advantages with the loss of the country's Arab character."

When President Roosevelt, in his talk with Ibn Saud early in 1945 suggested that there was room for many more millions in the vast undeveloped areas of the Arab countries and offered him support for reclamation projects, Ibn Saud is reported to have replied, "My people are of the desert; they are not interested in agriculture."

The same point of view was expressed at length in an article entitled *Palestine, the Arab Case,* in the Winter 1945 number of the London quarterly, *Courier,* pp. 56 and 57:

Since 1917 about 500,000 Jews have entered and settled in Palestine. It would be idle to deny that they have made many important economic changes in the country which, during the long centuries of its possession by the Turks, was in a state of progressive decay. The Jews have brought Western ideas of development with them. That is precisely a ground for Arab dissatisfaction and objection to the Jewish National Home in Palestine. The civilization of the Arabs is a different one from the West, in manners, custom and outlook. They have the right to determine their own way of life and the manner as well as the speed of their development. Arab ideas may be medieval; economically, their system may be feudal; they may be "behind the times" and live in the style of their forefathers, unwilling to become a part of what is called a progressive world. Nevertheless, these are the methods of their thought and life and it is within their right to follow them, if they are so minded.

The strength of this argument is undeniable. But so is that of the Jewish answer to it.

To the Arab nation, Palestine is only a small corner of the immense territories at its sole disposal. Iraq alone in Roman times held about twenty million inhabitants—today it has only three and a half millions. Irrigation and industrial development could bring back its former prosperity. And what of Arabia, Syria, the Lebanon, Egypt, North Africa? These vast territories, most of them undeveloped and underpopulated, offer ample opportunities for the growth and development of the Arab nation which, in fact, as a result of two world wars (in which it played, at best, a very insignificant part), achieved an increasing degree of independence and a free road to such unity as the Arabs themselves can attain. For the Jewish nation Palestine means the only chance of self-determination. In a Jewish Palestine the Arabs would have a com-

111

pletely equal status. This was carefully formulated by the first world Zionist conference to meet after the war, at London in August 1945. A resolution was there adopted which read:

(1) The Jewish State will be based upon full equality of rights of all inhabitants without distinction of religion or race in the political, civic, religious, and national domains, and without domination or subjection. All communities will enjoy full autonomy in the administration of their religious, educational, cultural, and social institutions. The Arabic language and Arab schools will enjoy full State rights. Municipal self-government will be developed in all towns and villages. The State will employ all efforts to raise and equalize the standard of living of all the inhabitants of Palestine.

(2) The Jewish people will aim at co-operating with the Arabs in Palestine in order to attain the highest degree of development of the country in the interests of all its inhabitants and will strive for an alliance of friendship between the Jewish State and the Arab peoples in the neighbouring countries, on the basis of reciprocal relations and mutual assistance for the welfare and progress of all countries in the Middle East.

Is the Arab nation under these circumstances really justified, for the sake of retaining the Arab character of the "small notch" of Palestine, in depriving the homeless Jewish nation of its only chance to regain its rightful place within the family of nations?

This would be a travesty of the right of national self-determination. For that right is neither unlimited nor unconditional. Here is a case where it must give way to a greater right, that of the Jewish nation which, not less than any other, is entitled to its own home where it can live in freedom and thus solve once and for all the problem of its very existence. As the Palestine Royal Commission put it:

It should also be remembered that the collective sufferings of Arabs and Jews are not comparable, since vast spaces in the Near East, formerly the abode of a numerous population and a home of a brilliant civilization, are open to the former, whereas the world is increasingly being closed to settlement by the latter.

Finally, when we speak of historical right, we must ask another question—what is history? When does the past begin? Is it only what lies far back, something that we, the living generation and our own parents did not see? And when does the concept of history begin, or rather when does it end in relation to our subject? This is by no means an academic question. For in the last sixty years or so, from the time of the immigration to Palestine of the so-called "Bilu" settlers to the present day, a very important, a decisive chapter has been written in the history of the relationship between the Jewish people and Palestine. Since the beginning of the eighties of the last century the Jewish people has demonstrated the deep and abiding character of its sense of connection with this land not only by prayer, not only by passive waiting, not only by

113

the upsurgings of sporadic messianic hopes and fitful attempts at immigration, but by systematic and increasing constructive activity. Zionism has by its concrete achievements strengthened the historic link between the people and the land, and has thus itself become a powerful factor in the creation of history and of historic right. This right was confirmed and sealed by the non-Jewish world in the Balfour Declaration and the Palestine Mandate, which, too, created rights. These are not merely formal rights, for in consequence of the issuance of the Declaration and the Mandate people and capital have been brought into Palestine, the whole face of the land has been transformed, and—what is not less important—the soul of the Jewish people has been changed, the way of thinking, of feeling and of behaving, of the Jewish people in Palestine and indeed throughout the world. All this creates rights, historical living rights.

The Jewish people's historical right to Palestine, we must conclude, derives its justification from the sufferings of an ancient people over a period of many generations and its unswerving, unforgetting yearning and hope; it has derived new strength through the sacrifice and achievement of two generations of pioneers, and through the earnest determination of the Jewish people to build its home in Palestine in peace and collaboration with its neighbor-nation.

CHRONOLOGICAL TABLE

B.C.

2000-1700 . . .	The Patriarchs
1250-1200 . . .	Moses; Exodus; Joshua; Conquest of Transjordan
1200-1000 . . .	The Judges; Samuel
1030-1010 . . .	Saul
1010-970	David; Jerusalem the capital of the entire Kingdom
970-930	Solomon; building of the Temple
930	Division of the Kingdom (Israel and Judah)
722	Sargon of Assyria conquers Samaria; deportation of the ten northern tribes
586	Nebuchadnezzar captures Jerusalem; destruction of the First Temple
538	The Cyrus Declaration; first Return from Babylon
520-516	The Temple rebuilt
458	The second Return (Ezra)
444	Proclamation of the Law by Ezra; Nehemiah rebuilds the walls of Jerusalem

116

Chronological Table

C.E.

4 C.E.	Judea a Roman province under procurators
40	The Jews defy Caligula
66-73	The Roman-Jewish War
70	The fall of Jerusalem; Jabneh Academy founded
73	The fall of Massada
115	Jewish revolt under Trajan
132-135	Revolt of Bar-Cochba
135-138	Persecution of the Jews under Hadrian
161	Revolt under Antonius Pius
201	Revolt under Septimius Severus
2nd and 3rd century	Immigration of Jews from Babylon
200	Conclusion of the Mishnah
352	Revolt under Constantine
362	Julian the Apostate orders the rebuilding of the Temple
400	Conclusion of the Palestinian Talmud. Jews and Samaritans still a majority in the country
429	Abolition of the Patriarchate
5th century	Pseudo-Messiah Moses of Crete
525	End of Jewish Kingdom in Southern Arabia
556	Jewish-Samaritan Revolt

117

578 . . . . Jewish-Samaritan Revolt

6th century . . . Justinian conquers the independent Jewish island of Jotaba (Tiran) in the Gulf of Akabah

602 . . . . Revolt of Jews in Antioch and probably also in Palestine under the Emperor Phocas

614 . . . . The Persians conquer Palestine, supported by a Jewish Army

624—5 . . . . . Mahomet expels Jewish tribes from Arabia to Southern Palestine

628 . . . . Heraclius reconquers Palestine

630 . . . . Mahomet concludes treaties with Jewish settlements in the south of Palestine.

636-638 . . . . The Arabs conquer Palestine

640 . . . . Omar I expels the Jews of Hedjaz to Tema (in Northern Arabia) and Jericho

7th and 8th
century . . . . . Completion of the text of the Bible; introduction of the vowel punctuation system

720 . . . . Pseudo-Messiah Serene of Syria

755 . . . . Pseudo-Messiah Abu-Isa of Ispahan

8th and 9th
century . . . . . Immigration of Jews from Babylon, Egypt and Syria into Palestine

118

800	Pseudo-Messiah Judah Judgan of Hamadan
10th century . .	Immigration of Jews from Africa and Spain into Palestine
1087	A pseudo-Messiah in France
1096	First Crusade; Jewish community in Palestine almost wiped out. Messianic emigration movement in Germany, South-eastern Europe and Khazaria
1099	The Crusaders capture Jerusalem
1117	A pseudo-Messiah in Spain
1121	A Karaite pseudo-Messiah in Palestine
1127	A pseudo-Messiah in Fez
1141	Yehuda Halevi's journey to Palestine
1160	Pseudo-Messiah David Alroy (Babylon)
1172	A pseudo-Messiah in Yemen
1187	Saladin conquers Palestine
1210	Three hundred French and English Rabbis settle in Palestine
1235	All Jews of Prague leave the city with the intention of starting for Palestine in expectation of the Messiah
1260	Syria and Palestine devastated by the Mongols; Jewish population greatly reduced
1267	Nahmanides settles in Palestine; rebuilds the Jewish community in Jerusalem

1284 . . . . . . Pseudo-Messiah Abraham Abulafia of Tudela (Spain)

1286 . . . . . . A large group of German Jews caught and punished for attempted secret emigration to Palestine

1392 . . . . . . A boat carrying Marranos on way to Palestine intercepted by Spanish authorities

1398 . . . . . . Pseudo-Messiah Moses Botarel of Castile

1455 . . . . . . Emigration movement from Sicily prevented

1482 . . . . . . Pope Martin V forbids Christian mariners to carry Jewish passengers to Palestine. The Doge of Venice issues similar order

1488 . . . . . . Obadia Bertinoro arrives in Palestine.

1492 . . . . . . Jews exiled from Spain and Portugal go to Palestine

1495 . . . . . . Several hundred Jews from Sicily immigrate into Palestine

End of 15th and
16th century . . Several thousand Jews from Spain, Portugal, Italy, etc., immigrate into Palestine

1502 . . . . . . Pseudo-Messiah Asher Laemlein (Germany)

1517 . . . . . . Palestine conquered by the Ottoman Turks

1522-1532 . . . Pseudo-Messiah David Reubeni

1529-1532 . . . Pseudo-Messiah Shlomo Molkho

1530 . . . . . . Palestine migration movement in Poland in connection with the appearance of Shlomo Molkho

1543 . . . . . . Pope Paul III orders population of Italy to render aid to Jews emigrating to Palestine

Middle 16th
century . . . . . Joseph Caro settles in Palestine

1560 . . . . . . Don Joseph Naxos begins rebuilding of Jewish settlement in Tiberias and environs

1581 . . . . . . Pope Gregory XIII repeats order of Pope Paul to aid Jews emigrating to Palestine

1621 . . . . . . Isaiah Halevi Hurvitz settles in Palestine. Beginning of the British movement for the restoration of the Jews

1665 . . . . . . Pseudo-Messiah Sabbatai Zevi

17th century . . Pseudo-Messiah Michael Cardozo (Spain)

1695 . . . . . . The Dane Holger Pauli submits to European Powers a plan for the restoration of the Jewish state

1700 . . . . . . 1,500 Jews from Poland, Hungary and Moravia emigrate to Palestine; 500 perish on the way

18th century . . Rabbi Shalom Sharabi (Yemen) settles in Palestine

1742 . . . . . . Rabbi Hayim ben Attar settles in Palestine

1744 . . . . . . Moshe Hayim Luzzatto, poet, Cabbalist and pseudo-Messiah, settles in Palestine.

1757 . . . . . . Pseudo-Messiah Jacob Frank (Poland)

1777 . . . . . . 300 Hassidim from Poland and their families immigrate into Palestine
Law drafted in Poland prohibiting Jewish emigration to Palestine

1799 . . . . . . Napoleon Bonaparte's call to the Jews on their restoration to Palestine

1812 . . . . . . 400 Lithuanian Jews immigrate into Palestine. Austrian Government takes steps to prevent Jewish emigration from Galicia to Palestine

1827 . . . . . . Sir Moses Montefiore's first journey to Palestine

1832-1840 . . . Palestine under Egyptian rule—Mohammed Ali

1836 . . . . . . Rabbi Zevi Hirsch Kalischer (Thorn, Germany) starts propaganda for Jewish colonization in Palestine

1840 . . . . . . Plan for Jewish restoration discussed by the European powers

Chronological Table

1840 . . . . . . The Damascus affair

1840 . . . . . . Palestine again under Turkish rule

1862 . . . . . . Appearance of Moses Hess's *Rome and Jerusalem*

1869 . . . . . . 400 Jews from Galicia and Bucovina emigrate into Palestine

1870 . . . . . . The agricultural school of Mikveh-Israel founded

1878 . . . . . . The first agricultural settlement "Petah Tikvah," founded

1882 . . . . . . Appearance of Leo Pinsker's *Auto-Emancipation*. Several hundred "Biluim" from Rusia immigrate into Palestine (beginning of "First Aliyah"). The settlements of Rishon LeZion, Ness-Ziona, Zikhron Jacob and Rosh-Pinah founded

1883 . . . . . . Turkish Government introduces "Red Certificate" limiting stay of newly arrived Jews in Palestine to three months

1892 . . . . . . Turkey prohibits the transfer of land to Jews from Russia, Rumania and Austria

1896 . . . . . . Publication of Herzl's *Jewish State*

1897 . . . . . . First Zionist World Congress — Zionist Organization created

1904-1914 . . . Second Aliyah

1909 . . . . . . Tel-Aviv founded

123

1911 . . . . . . The first collective settlement, "Degania," founded

1917 . . . . . . Balfour Declaration

1917-1918 . . . Palestine conquered by British Army

1918 . . . . . . A Jewish Legion takes part in the conquest of Palestine

1920 . . . . . . Beginning of Third Aliyah. Foundation of the General Federation of Jewish Labor in Palestine ("Histadrut")

1922 . . . . . . Confirmation of Palestine Mandate by Council of League of Nations; Transjordan closed to Jewish immigration

1924 . . . . . . Beginning of Fourth Aliyah.

1925 . . . . . . Foundation of Hebrew University

1929 . . . . . . Arab disturbances

1932 . . . . . . Fifth Aliyah

1936-1939 . . . Arab disturbances

1937 . . . . . . Royal Commission proposes partition of Palestine and creation of a Jewish State in a part of the country

1939 . . . . . . British White Paper virtually abolishes Balfour Declaration and purpose of Palestine Mandate; limits Jewish immigration to a final admittance of 75,000 immigrants in five years

1940 . . . . . . "Land Transfers Regulations" limit Jewish settlement to five per cent. of the country. First Palestinian Jewish units join the British Army

1944 . . . . . . A Brigade Group of Palestinian Jewish volunteers within the British Army take part in the liberation of Europe

1945 . . . . . . President Truman requests admission of 100,000 Displaced Jewish Persons to Palestine. Foreign Secretary Bevin suggests instead a joint Anglo-American Committee of Inquiry

1946 . . . . . . The Anglo-American Committee issues its report, which is rejected by the British Government. Mr. Truman welcomes its short-term recommendations, though reserving judgment on its long-term recommendation that Palestine be neither a Jewish nor an Arab state

1947 . . . . . . After the failure of talks with the Arabs and Jews, the British Government turns the Palestine issue over to the United Nations. A special session of the General Assembly is held and appoints a U.N. Committee of Investigation

AUTHOR

Locker, B.

TITLE

Covenant everlasting.

DATE LOANED	BORROWER'S NAME	DATE RETURNED
1/15/5?	Louis F. Knoll	√
4/9/5	Broadbriel	

DATE LOANED	BORROWER'S NAME	DATE RETURNED

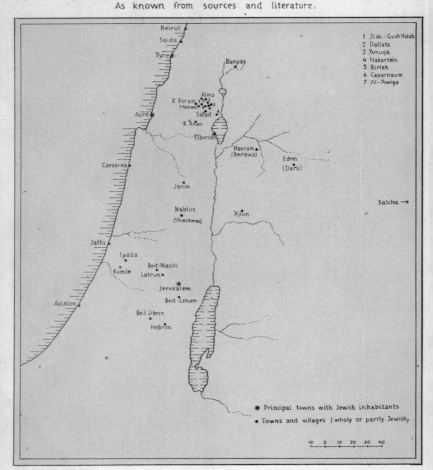

PALESTINE
JEWISH SETTLEMENTS DURING THE CRUSADER PERIOD 1099 – 1291
As known from sources and literature.

1 Jish - Gush Halab
2 Dallata
3 'Amuqa
4 Nabartein
5 Biriah
6 Caparnaum
7 Al-'Awiya

Beirut
Saida
Tyre
Banyas
Alma
K. Biram
Meron
Safad
Acre
K. 'Anan
Tiberias
Havram
(Amrawa)
Edrei
(Dara)
Caesarea
Salcha →
Jenin
Nablus
(Shechem)
'Ajlun
Jaffa
Lydda
Beit-Naubi
Ramle
Latrun
Jerusalem
Ascalon
Beit-Lehem
Beit Jibrin
Hebron

● Principal towns with Jewish inhabitants
• Towns and villages (wholly or partly Jewish)

10   0   10   20   30   40